Target
Get back on track

AQA GCSE (9–1)
English Literature
Romeo and Juliet

Julie Hughes

Published by Pearson Education Limited, 80 Strand, London, WC2R 0RL.
www.pearsonschoolsandfecolleges.co.uk

Text © Pearson Education Ltd 2018
Produced and typeset by QBS Learning

The right of Julie Hughes to be identified as author of this work has been asserted by her in accordance with the Copyright, Designs and Patents Act 1988.

First published 2018

21 20 19 18
10 9 8 7 6 5 4 3 2 1

British Library Cataloguing in Publication Data
A catalogue record for this book is available from the British Library

ISBN 978 1 292 25080 9

Copyright notice
All rights reserved. No part of this publication may be reproduced in any form or by any means (including photocopying or storing it in any medium by electronic means and whether or not transiently or incidentally to some other use of this publication) without the written permission of the copyright owner, except in accordance with the provisions of the Copyright, Designs and Patents Act 1988 or under the terms of a licence issued by the Copyright Licensing Agency, Barnard's Inn, 86 Fetter Lane, London EC4A 1EN (www.cla.co.uk). Applications for the copyright owner's written permission should be addressed to the publisher.

Printed in Slovakia by Neografia

Notes from the publisher
Pearson has robust editorial processes, including answer and fact checks, to ensure the accuracy of the content in this publication, and every effort is made to ensure this publication is free of errors. We are, however, only human, and occasionally errors do occur. Pearson is not liable for any misunderstandings that arise as a result of errors in this publication, but it is our priority to ensure that the content is accurate. If you spot an error, please do contact us at resourcescorrections@pearson.com so we can make sure it is corrected.

Contents

1 Getting the plot straight
Get started — 1
1 How do I make sure I know the plot? — 3
2 How can I explore the development of the plot? — 4
3 How do I know which are the most significant events in the play? — 5
Get back on track — 6

2 Analysing the extract
Get started — 9
1 How do I choose the points I need to make? — 11
2 How do I develop my analysis? — 12
3 How do I structure a paragraph of analysis? — 13
Get back on track — 14

3 Commenting on the writer's choices in the extract
Get started — 17
1 How do I identify significant language choices? — 19
2 How do I identify significant structural choices? — 20
3 How do I comment on the writer's choices? — 21
Get back on track — 22

4 Exploring themes and characters
Get started — 25
1 How do I track the development of a character? — 27
2 How do I track the development of a theme? — 28
3 How do I comment on the development of character or theme? — 29
Get back on track — 30

5 Planning your response
Get started — 33
1 How do I make a critical judgement? — 35
2 How do I gather relevant points? — 36
3 How do I sequence my points? — 37
Get back on track — 38

6 Writing your response
Get started — 41
1 How do I choose key events and key quotations to learn? — 43
2 How do I use evidence to support my ideas? — 44
3 How do I analyse my evidence? — 45
Get back on track — 46

7 Commenting on the structure of the play
Get started — 49
1 How can I comment on the structure of the play? — 51
2 How do I comment on the impact of structure? — 52
3 How do I analyse the writer's use of structure? — 53
Get back on track — 54

8 Commenting on context
Get started — 57
1 How do I know which contextual ideas to write about? — 59
2 How do I comment on context? — 60
3 How do I build my comments on context into my analysis? — 61
Get back on track — 62

9 Developing a critical writing style
Get started — 65
1 How do I choose vocabulary that expresses my ideas precisely? — 67
2 How can I link my ideas to express them more clearly? — 68
3 How can I extend my sentences to develop my ideas more fully? — 69
Get back on track — 70

More practice questions — 73
Answers — 78

Get started Read, understand and respond to texts (AO1)

① Getting the plot straight

This unit will help you to understand and remember the plot of *Romeo and Juliet*. The skills you will build are to:

- remember the sequence of key events in the play
- understand the causes and consequences of the key events in the play
- understand what makes some events in the play more significant than others.

In the exam you will face questions like the one below. This is about the extract on the next page. At the end of the unit you will **plan your own response** to this question.

> **Exam-style question**
>
> Starting with this extract, explore how Shakespeare presents attitudes to conflict in *Romeo and Juliet*.
>
> Write about:
> - how Shakespeare presents attitudes to conflict in this extract
> - how Shakespeare presents attitudes to conflict in the play as a whole.
>
> (30 marks)
> AO4 (4 marks)

Before you tackle the question you will work through three key questions in the **skills boosts** to help you to get the plot of *Romeo and Juliet* straight.

① How do I make sure I know the plot?

② How can I explore the development of the plot?

③ How do I know which are the most significant events in the play?

Read the extract on the next page from Act 1 Scene 1 of *Romeo and Juliet*.

As you read, think about the following:

- Where in the play does this scene appear? Is it near the beginning, in the middle or at the end?
- What has happened before this scene? What happens after this scene?
- Why is the conflict in this scene important?

Unit 1 Getting the plot straight   1

Get started

> **Exam-style question**
>
> Read the following extract from Act 1 Scene 1 of *Romeo and Juliet*.
>
> At this point in the play an argument between Capulet and Montague servants develops into a fight. Benvolio, a Montague, attempts to stop the fighting before Tybalt and Lord and Lady Capulet arrive.

Extract A | Act 1 Scene 1 of *Romeo and Juliet*

SAMPSON
Draw, if you be men! Gregory, remember thy washing blow!
They fight.
BENVOLIO draws his sword and tries to separate them.
BENVOLIO
Part, fools!
Put up your swords! You know not what you do.
Enter TYBALT.
TYBALT
What, art thou drawn among these heartless hinds?
5 Turn thee, Benvolio! Look upon thy death.
BENVOLIO
I do but keep the peace! Put up thy sword
Or manage it to part these men with me.
TYBALT
What, drawn, and talk of peace? I hate the word
As I hate hell, all Montagues, and thee.
10 Have at thee, coward!
They fight.
Enter a city OFFICER, with three or four armed citizens, who rush in to try to stop the fighting.
OFFICER
Clubs, bills, and partisans! Strike! Beat them down!
Down with the Capulets! Down with the Montagues!
Enter old CAPULET, in his dressing-gown, followed by LADY CAPULET, his wife.
CAPULET
What noise is this? Give me my long sword, ho!

Unit 1 Getting the plot straight

Skills boost

1 How do I make sure I know the plot?

One way to make sure you know the plot of *Romeo and Juliet* is to focus on the characters and how they react to each other in the play.

Look at this list of the main characters in the play. Use it to help you answer the questions below.

Escalus, Prince of Verona ☐	Lady Montague ☐	Juliet ☐
Paris ☐	Mercutio ☐	Lady Montague ☐
Lord Montague ☐	Tybalt ☐	Lady Capulet ☐
Lord Capulet ☐	Friar Lawrence ☐	Friar John ☐
Romeo ☐	Sampson ☐	Gregory ☐
Benvolio ☐	Nurse ☐	Abraham ☐

1. The background to the play is the feud between the Montagues and the Capulets.

   a. Label each character: M = Montague, C = Capulet or N = neutral.

   b. Several characters are killed during fights in the play. Cross out their names, then draw a line from each deleted name to the character who kills them.

2. The play takes place over the course of only four days, from Sunday morning to Thursday morning.

   a. How many times do Romeo and Juliet actually meet during this time? Circle the correct answer.

   | five times | six times | three times |

   b. What happens at the start of the play on Sunday morning? Write your answer in the correct box in the plot summary below.

   c. What happens at the end of the play?

   d. Add Romeo and Juliet's meetings and all the deaths to the plot summary.

	Sunday	Monday	Tuesday	Wednesday	Thursday
Day					
Night					

   e. Now that you have listed the meetings and the deaths, can you add any further details about where Romeo and Juliet meet, or why/how people die?

Unit 1 Getting the plot straight

Skills boost

2 How can I explore the development of the plot?

Understanding the causes and consequences of key events in *Romeo and Juliet* will help you to get the plot straight and help you to understand how the plot develops.

Look at some of the key events in *Romeo and Juliet*.

Causes   Consequences

1.1	The Prince stops a street fight between the two families, warning that anybody caught disturbing the peace in future will face execution.
1.2	Benvolio persuades Romeo to go to the ball and test his feelings for Rosaline.
1.3	Juliet's mother urges her to marry Paris.
1.5	Romeo and Juliet fall in love at first sight before finding out they are from opposing families.
2.6	Romeo and Juliet are married in secret by Friar Lawrence.
3.1	Mercutio and Tybalt are killed in a street fight.
3.1	Benvolio is questioned about the fight and Romeo is banished.
3.4	Capulet promises Juliet in marriage to Paris.
3.5	Romeo and Juliet secretly spend the night together.
3.5	Juliet refuses to marry Paris so her father threatens to disown her.
4.1	Friar Lawrence comes up with a plan to help Juliet.
5.2	Friar Lawrence's plan fails when his message does not get to Romeo.
5.3	Romeo kills Paris then kills himself by taking poison.
5.3	Juliet wakes, sees Romeo is dead and kills herself.
5.3	The Montagues and Capulets decide to end their feud.

(1) One of the key events in the play is the **killing of Mercutio and Tybalt**.

   a On the left of the list above, draw arrows ⬇ to show the chain of **causes** that leads to the **killings**.

   b On the right-hand side, draw arrows ⬇ to show the chain of **consequences** caused by the **killings**.

   c Annotate 🖉 your links with ideas about how the events caused the killings of Mercutio and Tybalt and how their deaths affected the later events you chose as consequences.

> One arrow for cause and one arrow for consequence have already been drawn for you to start the chain.

(2) Choose another significant event in the play and underline Ⓐ it. Consider how it contributes to the deaths of Romeo and Juliet. Draw arrows ⬇ in a different colour to explore the **causes** and **consequences** of the event you have chosen.

Unit 1 Getting the plot straight

Skills boost

3 How do I know which are the most significant events in the play?

Understanding what each key event contributes to the play will help you to get the plot straight and identify significant parts of the play to write about in your responses.

Look at some of the key events in *Romeo and Juliet*.

Mark out of 5 ✓

1.1	The Prince stops a street fight between the two families, warning that anybody caught disturbing the peace in future will face execution.	☐	☐
1.2	Benvolio persuades Romeo to go to the ball and test his feelings for Rosaline.	☐	☐
1.3	Juliet's mother urges her to marry Paris.	☐	☐
1.5	Romeo and Juliet fall in love at first sight before finding out they are from opposing families.	☐	☐
2.6	Romeo and Juliet are married in secret by Friar Lawrence.	☐	☐
3.1	Mercutio and Tybalt are killed in a street fight.	☐	☐
3.1	Benvolio is questioned about the fight and Romeo is banished.	☐	☐
3.4	Capulet promises Juliet in marriage to Paris.	☐	☐
3.5	Romeo and Juliet secretly spend the night together.	☐	☐
3.5	Juliet refuses to marry Paris so her father threatens to disown her.	☐	☐
4.1	Friar Lawrence comes up with a plan to help Juliet.	☐	☐
5.2	Friar Lawrence's plan fails when his message does not get to Romeo.	☐	☐
5.3	Romeo kills Paris then kills himself by taking poison.	☐	☐
5.3	Juliet wakes, sees Romeo is dead and kills herself.	☐	☐
5.3	The Montagues and Capulets decide to end their feud.	☐	☐

(1) Write ✏️ **one** sentence explaining how the story would change if Shakespeare had decided to let Mercutio survive the fight with Tybalt. ....

....

(2) Now, think carefully about each of the key events listed above. For each one, ask yourself:

> ❓ How would the play's ending change if it were removed?

> ❓ How relevant is it to a question about attitudes to conflict?

- **a** Beside each key event, note down ✏️ a mark out of 5: give it 5 if its removal would change the ending significantly and 1 if its removal would not affect the ending very much.
- **b** Tick ✓ the **three** events that you think are most relevant to a question about attitudes to conflict. Annotate ✏️ each one, noting why you have decided it is so significant.

Unit 1 Getting the plot straight

Getting the plot straight

Get back on track

To be sure of writing an effective response about *Romeo and Juliet*, you need to:
- know the key events in the play and the order in which they happen
- understand the causes and consequences of the key events in the play
- be able to identify the most relevant events to use in a response.

Look again at the **first** part of the exam-style question you saw at the start of the unit.

Exam-style question

Starting with this extract, explore how Shakespeare presents attitudes to conflict in *Romeo and Juliet*.

Write about:
- how Shakespeare presents attitudes to conflict in this extract

(1) Now look at one student's planning notes, written in response to this exam-style question.

Before this scene: Prologue tells audience about feud and suggests it causes deaths of R & J.

After this scene: Prince warns that any future fighting will end in execution.

So conflict is very important in this scene as it establishes what will happen if the families continue with their feud.

In the extract:
Shows that attitudes to conflict are the same through all levels of society as servants start the violence: 'Draw if you be men!', and Capulet wants to join in: 'Give me my long sword!'
'if you be men' suggests sword fighting is seen as an honourable way to deal with conflict.
Benvolio stands out as different as he appears to look down on the conflict: 'Part, fools!'.
Tybalt contrasts with Benvolio, calling him a 'coward'.

Think about all the ideas this student has included in their plan. Annotate their plan, highlighting all the different elements that will make their response to the first part of the question above successful.

Unit 1 Getting the plot straight

Get back on track

Your turn!

After you have read and understood the text, identified its key points and explored the writer's intention, you are ready to tackle **all of the questions** you are likely to be asked in your exam.

You are now going to **plan your own answer** in response to the exam-style question.

Exam-style question

Starting with this extract, explore how Shakespeare presents attitudes to conflict in *Romeo and Juliet*.

Write about:
- how Shakespeare presents attitudes to conflict in this extract
- how Shakespeare presents attitudes to conflict in the play as a whole.

1 Look again at some of the key events in the play.

		✓	✗
1.2	Benvolio persuades Romeo to go to the ball and test his feelings for Rosaline.		
1.3	Juliet's mother urges her to marry Paris.		
1.5	Romeo and Juliet fall in love at first sight before finding out they are from opposing families.		
2.6	Romeo and Juliet are married in secret by Friar Lawrence.		
3.1	Mercutio and Tybalt are killed in a street fight.		
3.1	Benvolio is questioned about the fight and Romeo is banished.		
3.4	Capulet promises Juliet in marriage to Paris.		
3.5	Romeo and Juliet secretly spend the night together.		
3.5	Juliet refuses to marry Paris so her father threatens to disown her.		
4.1	Friar Lawrence comes up with a plan to help Juliet.		
5.2	Friar Lawrence's plan fails when his message does not get to Romeo.		
5.3	Romeo kills Paris then kills himself by taking poison.		
5.3	Juliet wakes, sees Romeo is dead and kills herself.		
5.3	The Montagues and Capulets decide to end their feud.		

a Which key events are not relevant to a question about conflict? Cross ✗ them.
b Which key events show different attitudes to conflict? Tick ✓ them.
c Annotate ✏ **two** of your choices to explain the attitude to conflict that is shown.
d How many different types of conflict are represented by your choices? Annotate ✏ each one to show what type of conflict it represents.

Unit 1 Getting the plot straight

Get back on track

Review your skills

Check up

Review your plan for the exam-style question on page 7. Tick ✓ the column to show how well you think you have done each of the following.

	Not quite ✓	Nearly there ✓	Got it! ✓
shown an understanding of the sequence of events in the play	☐	☐	☐
shown an understanding of the causes and consequences of conflict in the play	☐	☐	☐
identified the most relevant key events to explore attitudes to conflict in the play	☐	☐	☐

Look over all of your work in this unit. Note down ✏ the **three** most important things to remember when selecting key scenes for a *Romeo and Juliet* question.

1. ....
2. ....
3. ....

Need more practice?

Here is another exam-style question, this time relating to the extract from Act 5 Scene 3 on page 73 (Extract A).

Exam-style question

Starting with this extract, explore how Shakespeare presents feelings of anguish in *Romeo and Juliet*.

Write about:
- how Shakespeare presents feelings of anguish in this speech
- how Shakespeare presents feelings of anguish in the play as a whole.

(30 marks)
AO4 (4 marks)

Which key events in the play would you choose to write ✏ about in your response to this question? You'll find some suggested ideas in the Answers section.

How confident do you feel about each of these **skills**? Colour ✏ in the bars.

1 How do I make sure I know the plot?

2 How can I explore the development of the plot?

3 How do I know which are the most significant events in the play?

Unit 1 Getting the plot straight

Get started
Read, understand and respond to texts (AO1)

② Analysing the extract

This unit will help you to explore the extract in the *Romeo and Juliet* exam question. The skills you will build are to:

- select relevant points to make in your analysis
- develop your analysis
- structure your analysis.

In the exam you will face questions like the one below. This is about the extract on the next page. At the end of the unit you will **write one paragraph** in response to this question, **focusing on the extract**.

Exam-style question

Starting with this extract, explore how Shakespeare presents ideas about fate in *Romeo and Juliet*.

Write about:
- how Shakespeare presents ideas about fate in this extract
- how Shakespeare presents ideas about fate in the play as a whole.

(30 marks)
AO4 (4 marks)

Before you tackle the question you will work through three key questions in the **skills boosts** to help you analyse the extract.

1. How do I choose the points I need to make?
2. How do I develop my analysis?
3. How do I structure a paragraph of analysis?

Read the extract on the next page from Act 3 Scene 5 of *Romeo and Juliet*.

As you read, think about the following:

- What has happened before this scene? What happens after this scene?
- How does Shakespeare present fate in this extract?
- How does Shakespeare present Romeo and Juliet's relationship in this extract?

Unit 2 Analysing the extract 9

Get started

> **Exam-style question**
>
> Read the following extract from Act 3 Scene 5 of *Romeo and Juliet*.
>
> At this point in the play Romeo is about to leave Juliet to travel to Mantua as he has been banished. Juliet has tried to persuade him to stay but realises that to do so is too dangerous.

Extract A | Act 3 Scene 5 of *Romeo and Juliet*

JULIET
Art thou gone so, love? – lord, ay husband, friend!
I must hear from thee every day in the hour,
For in a minute there are many days.
O, by this count I shall be much in years
5   Ere I again behold my Romeo!
ROMEO
(From the garden below) Farewell! I will omit no opportunity
That may convey my greetings, love, to thee.
JULIET
O think'st thou we shall ever meet again?
ROMEO
I doubt it not. And all these woes shall serve
10 For sweet discourses in our time to come.
JULIET
O God, I have an ill-divining soul!
Methinks I see thee, now thou art so low,
As one dead in the bottom of a tomb.
Either my eyesight fails, or thou look'st pale.
ROMEO
15 And trust me, love, in my eye so do you.
Dry sorrow drinks our blood. Adieu, adieu!
Exit ROMEO.
JULIET pulls up the rope-ladder.
JULIET
O Fortune, Fortune! All men call thee fickle.
If thou art fickle, what dost thou with him
That is renowned for faith? *Be* fickle, Fortune –
20 For then I hope thou wilt not keep him long,
But send him back.
LADY CAPULET
(From inside the house) Ho, daughter, are you up?

Skills boost

1. How do I choose the points I need to make?

The first thing you need to do is to identify which parts of the extract you can explore further in your response to the question.

Look at the focus of the exam-style question and think about the key words. Here, the focus is fate:

Exam-style question

Starting with this extract, explore how Shakespeare presents <u>ideas about fate</u> in *Romeo and Juliet*.

(1) Now look through the extract on page 10, focusing on each speech in turn

1	Juliet regrets that Romeo must go and says she must hear from him regularly. [lines 1–5]	☐
2	Romeo says he will send his love often. [lines 6–7]	☐
3	Juliet wonders if they will ever meet again and Romeo reassures her that they will. [lines 8–10]	☐
4	Juliet says she is a pessimist and thinks she can see Romeo's death. [lines 11–14]	☐
5	Romeo says goodbye and leaves. [lines 15–16]	☐
6	Juliet hopes fortune will allow Romeo to return to her. [lines 17–21]	☐
7	Juliet's mother enters the room and calls for Juliet. [line 22]	☐

a Decide which **three** sections reveal the most about how Shakespeare presents ideas about fate.
Label ✎ them A, B and C.

Think about:
- what effect fate has on the characters' feelings
- whether fate is presented as positive or negative.

b Note ✎ below what each of the sections you have chosen reveals about how Shakespeare presents ideas about fate.

A

B

C

Unit 2 Analysing the extract   11

Skills boost

2 How do I develop my analysis?

To develop your analysis, you need to think about what the characters say, why they say it, and what this reveals about the aspect of the play that you are exploring. Your ideas need to be supported by evidence from the extract.

Look again at the exam-style question you are considering.

Exam-style question

Starting with this extract, explore how Shakespeare presents ideas about fate in *Romeo and Juliet*.

1 Now look at these short sections from the extract and think about what each reveals about fate.

> **JULIET**
> O think'st thou we shall ever meet again?
>
> **ROMEO**
> I doubt it not. And all these woes shall serve
> For sweet discourses in our time to come.
>
> **JULIET**
> O God, I have an ill-divining soul!
>
> Methinks I see thee, now thou art so low,
>
> As one dead in the bottom of a tomb.
>
> Either my eyesight fails, or thou look'st pale.

   a For each section of dialogue, write 🖉 in your own words what each character means in the box next to it.

   b Sum up 🖉 the conversation in **one** sentence.

   ....
   ....

   c Look again at your answers above. What does this conversation suggest about the way fate affects the characters in the play? 🖉

   ....
   ....
   ....

   d Which lines show this most clearly? Choose **two** short quotations and underline Ⓐ them.

2 Now look at lines 17–21 from the extract.

   a Annotate 🖉 the text on page 10, noting down:
   - what Juliet says
   - why she says it
   - what ideas it reveals about fate.

   b Then underline Ⓐ **two** short quotations to support your ideas.

Unit 2 Analysing the extract

Skills boost

3 How do I structure a paragraph of analysis?

Each paragraph of your analysis should include:
- a key point focusing on the key words in the question
- evidence from the text to support your point
- comments on the evidence and its impact
- a response to the question.

> You can build your skill in analysing the extract in more depth and detail in Unit 3.

Look at the sentences from one paragraph of a student's response to this exam-style question.

Exam-style question

Starting with this extract, explore how Shakespeare presents ideas about fate in *Romeo and Juliet*.

(1) Tick ✓ the sentences you would include in a paragraph in response to the exam-style question.

A	Juliet has a vision of Romeo's death: 'Methinks I see thee, now thou art so low,/As one dead in the bottom of a tomb.'	
B	Juliet feels that fate is controlling their lives.	
C	Ideas about fate in 'Romeo and Juliet' are linked to death.	
D	Shakespeare presents fate as something very negative.	
E	Shakespeare has used fate in this scene.	
F	Juliet is worried that her vision is going to come true as she thinks Romeo 'look'st pale'.	

(2) How would you sequence your chosen sentences in a paragraph? Number ✎ them.

(3) Write ✎ a paragraph using your chosen sentences and linking them with some or all of the following phrases.

| Also, | This shows that | It suggests that | For example, | This emphasises that |

....
....
....
....

(4) Look at the sentences you have chosen and sequenced.
  a Which make a key point? Label ✎ them 'Key point'.
  b Which support a key point using evidence? Label ✎ them 'Evidence'.
  c Which comment on the evidence and its impact? Label ✎ them 'Comment'.
  d Which show a response to the question? Label ✎ them 'Response'.

Unit 2 Analysing the extract

Get back on track

Analysing the extract

To analyse the extract effectively, you need to:
- identify the parts of the extract that are relevant to the question
- explore what these parts suggest about the focus of the question
- structure your paragraphs of analysis to include a key point supported by evidence, a comment on its impact and a response to the question.

Look at the exam-style question you saw at the start of the unit.

Exam-style question

Starting with this extract, explore how Shakespeare presents ideas about fate in *Romeo and Juliet*.

(1) Look at this paragraph, taken from a student's response to this question. It focuses on the extract on page 10, Extract A.

> In this extract, where Romeo and Juliet say goodbye as he has been banished, they are shown to have different reactions to the role of fate in their lives. Romeo is presented as the more positive of the lovers as he tries to reassure Juliet that their 'woes' will turn into 'sweet discourses in our time to come', suggesting that he believes he has some control over their future. Juliet, on the other hand, is more negative and links fate to death by talking of a vision of Romeo 'As one dead in the bottom of a tomb'. This suggests that Romeo's death is his destiny and nothing can stop it happening, which presents fate as something controlling the characters' lives.

(a) Which of the following has this student achieved? Tick ✓ them.

A	Shown an understanding of where the extract fits into the plot.	☐
B	Identified parts of the extract that are relevant to the question.	☐
C	Made a key point.	☐
D	Supported it with evidence.	☐
E	Commented on its impact.	☐
F	Responded to the question.	☐

(b) Highlight and label ✎ where in the paragraph this student has achieved A–F.

Get back on track

Your turn!

You are now going to **write one paragraph** in response to the exam-style question below, **focusing on Juliet's final speech and her mother's entrance** in Extract A on page 10.

> **JULIET**
> O Fortune, Fortune! All men call thee fickle.
> If thou art fickle, what dost thou with him
> That is renowned for faith? *Be* fickle, Fortune –
> For then I hope thou wilt not keep him long,
> But send him back.
> **LADY CAPULET**
> *(From inside the house)* Ho, daughter, are you up?

Exam-style question

Starting with this extract, explore how Shakespeare presents ideas about fate in *Romeo and Juliet*.

Write about:
- how Shakespeare presents ideas about fate in this extract
- how Shakespeare presents ideas about fate in the play as a whole.

(30 marks)
AO4 (4 marks)

1. Look at Juliet's speech. What is she saying about fortune?

2. What does this suggest about Juliet's feelings about fate?

3. Juliet's mother interrupts her speech. What does this suggest about the role of fate in Juliet's life?

4. Underline (A) short, relevant quotations above that you can use in your response.

5. On paper, write one paragraph in response to the exam-style question above.

Unit 2 Analysing the extract

Review your skills

Check up

Review your response to the exam-style question on page 15. Tick ✓ the column to show how well you think you have done each of the following.

	Not quite ✓	Nearly there ✓	Got it! ✓
made a relevant key point	☐	☐	☐
supported my key point with relevant evidence	☐	☐	☐
commented on the impact of my evidence	☐	☐	☐
responded to the question	☐	☐	☐

Look over all of your work in this unit. Note down three pieces of advice on how to analyse an extract.

1. ....
2. ....
3. ....

Need more practice?

Here is another exam-style question, this time relating to the extract from Act 5 Scene 3 on page 73 (Extract A).

Exam-style question

Starting with this extract, explore how Shakespeare presents feelings of anguish in *Romeo and Juliet*.

Write about:
- how Shakespeare presents feelings of anguish in this speech
- how Shakespeare presents feelings of anguish in the play as a whole.

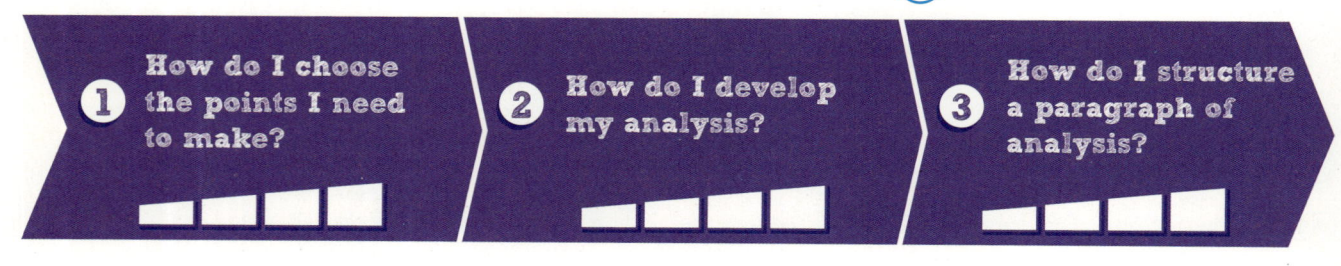

(30 marks)
AO4 (4 marks)

Write one or two paragraphs in response to this question, focusing on the extract only.

You'll find some suggested ideas in the Answers section.

How confident do you feel about each of these **skills?** Colour in the bars.

1 How do I choose the points I need to make?

2 How do I develop my analysis?

3 How do I structure a paragraph of analysis?

Get started

Analyse the language, form and structure used by a writer to create meanings and effects (AO2)

③ Commenting on the writer's choices in the extract

This unit will help you to comment on Shakespeare's choices in the extract from *Romeo and Juliet*. The skills you will build are to:

- identify relevant language choices to comment on
- identify relevant structural choices to comment on
- make effective comments on the writer's choices.

In the exam you will face questions like the one below. This is about the extract on the next page. At the end of the unit you will **write one or two paragraphs** in response to this question, **focusing on the extract**.

> **Exam-style question**
>
> Starting with this extract, how does Shakespeare present romantic love in *Romeo and Juliet*?
>
> Write about:
> - how Shakespeare presents romantic love in this extract
> - how Shakespeare presents romantic love in the play as a whole.
>
> (30 marks)
> AO4 (4 marks)

Before you tackle the question you will work through three key questions in the **skills boosts** to help you comment on the writer's choices in the extract.

① How do I identify significant language choices?
② How do I identify significant structural choices?
③ How do I comment on the writer's choices?

Read the extract on the next page from Act 1 Scene 1 of *Romeo and Juliet*.

As you read, think about the following:

- What has happened before this scene? What happens after this scene?
- How does Shakespeare present Romeo and Benvolio in this extract?
- How does Shakespeare present romantic love in this extract?

Unit 3 Commenting on the writer's choices in the extract   17

Get started

> **Exam-style question**
>
> Read the following extract from Act 1 Scene 1 of *Romeo and Juliet*.
>
> At this point in the play Benvolio questions Romeo about what is wrong with him. Romeo explains that he has fallen in love.

Extract A | Act 1 Scene 1 of *Romeo and Juliet*

BENVOLIO
… What sadness lengthens Romeo's hours?

ROMEO
Not having that, which, having, makes them short.

BENVOLIO
In love?

ROMEO
Out –

BENVOLIO
5   Of love?

ROMEO
Out of her favour where I am in love.

BENVOLIO
Alas, that Love, so gentle in his view,
Should be so tyrannous and rough in proof!

ROMEO
Alas, that Love, whose view is muffled still,
10   Should without eyes see pathways to his will!
Where shall we dine? O me! What fray was here?
Yet tell me not, for I have heard it all.
Here's much to do with hate, but more with love.
Why then, O brawling love, O loving hate,
15   O anything of nothing first create!
O heavy lightness, serious vanity,
Misshapen chaos of well-seeming forms!
Feather of lead, bright smoke, cold fire, sick health,
Still-waking sleep, that is not what it is!
20   This love feel I, that feel no love in this.
Dost thou not laugh?

BENVOLIO
          No, coz, I rather weep.

ROMEO
Good heart, at what?

BENVOLIO
          At *thy* good heart's oppression.

Skills boost

1 How do I identify significant language choices?

The language that Shakespeare gives each character in a scene or extract can reveal a great deal about their thoughts, motivations and relationships.

1 When considering significant language choices, it is helpful to think about the connotations, or hidden meanings, of the words and phrases used. For example, in his speech below, Benvolio suggests love is 'gentle' to look at. The word 'gentle' suggests love can be:

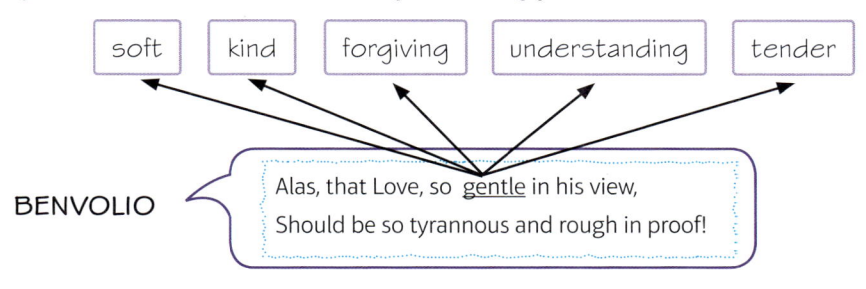

soft | kind | forgiving | understanding | tender

BENVOLIO: Alas, that Love, so gentle in his view,
Should be so tyrannous and rough in proof!

a Which words does Shakespeare give Benvolio to suggest love is actually cruel? Circle your choices.

b Now choose **one** of your words and note down all its connotations.

Word chosen: ....

Connotations: ....

c What does Shakespeare's choice of words and phrases suggest about love? Write **one** sentence to explain your ideas about their connotations.

....

....

2 Now consider Shakespeare's choice of language techniques by considering some of Romeo's response to Benvolio's statement about love.

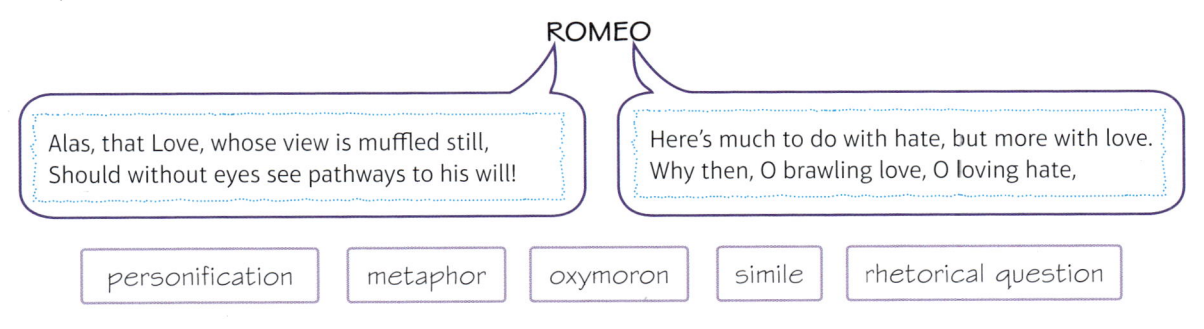

ROMEO:
Alas, that Love, whose view is muffled still,
Should without eyes see pathways to his will!

Here's much to do with hate, but more with love.
Why then, O brawling love, O loving hate,

personification | metaphor | oxymoron | simile | rhetorical question

personification: giving human attributes to inanimate objects
metaphor: comparison directly equating two things
oxymoron: juxtaposing opposite ideas or apparent contradictions
simile: indirect comparison using 'like' or 'as'
rhetorical question: question posed for effect, not requiring a response

Try to use the correct subject terminology for the language and techniques you select.

a Which of the above language techniques has Shakespeare used in Romeo's speech? Circle your choices and draw an arrow to where each choice appears in the speech.

b Now think about what your selections suggest about the character of Romeo or the nature of romantic love. Pick one of your choices from question a and annotate it with your ideas.

Unit 3 Commenting on the writer's choices in the extract

Skills boost

2 How do I identify significant structural choices?

When you think about Shakespeare's structural choices, you must remember that *Romeo and Juliet* is a play. This means you should consider:

- the length and position of lines in the extract
- what type of speech is used for each line.

1 Look at these lines from the extract.

> **BENVOLIO**
> … What sadness lengthens Romeo's hours?
> **ROMEO**
> Not having that which, having, makes them short.
> **BENVOLIO**
> In love?
> **ROMEO**
> Out –
> **BENVOLIO**
> Of love?

a What does this conversation suggest about Romeo, Benvolio, their friendship and romantic love?

Link 🖉 **one** or **two** of the following ideas to each bullet point below, or add 🖉 your own.

| sympathetic | close | brotherly | sulky | gloomy |
| despondent | kind | affectionate | difficult | painful |

- Romeo
- Benvolio
- friendship
- romantic love

b How does the **length** of the lines, the **position** of the lines, and the **pace** at which the actors might deliver them, create ideas about the characters, their relationship and the theme of romantic love? Write 🖉 **one** or **two** sentences explaining your ideas.

....
....

2 Shakespeare changes the style of language throughout the play to give the audience ideas about characters and themes. For instance, for important speeches, blank verse with some rhyming couplets is used to emphasise key points for the audience.

a In this extract, who is given blank verse with rhyming couplets? 🖉 ....

b What does this speech pattern suggest about the character's mood? 🖉
....
....

c Which character's lines are mostly like ordinary speech? 🖉 ....

d What does this type of speech pattern suggest about the character? 🖉
....

Unit 3 Commenting on the writer's choices in the extract

Skills boost

3 How do I comment on the writer's choices?

An effective comment on Shakespeare's choices highlights the **choice** the writer has made, and comments on its **effect**.

Look at some of the different comments on **language** and **structure** you could make about the following part of Romeo's speech.

Romeo
> Why then, O brawling love, O loving hate,
> O anything of nothing first create!
> O heavy lightness, serious vanity,
> Misshapen chaos of well-seeming forms!
> Feather of lead, bright smoke, cold fire, sick health,
> Still-waking sleep, that is not what it is!
> This love feel I, that feel no love in this.
> Dost thou not laugh?

Evidence

A The emotive verb 'brawling'…

B The oxymoron 'Feather of lead'…

C The personification 'O brawling love'…

D The final short line of the scene 'Dost thou not laugh?'…

E The final rhyming couplet 'is' and 'this'…

Comment

a … suggests he is embarrassed about the strength of his feelings as it comes after a long speech.

b … has connotations of a rough, noisy type of fight.

c … emphasises that he is finding this extreme state of love very hard.

d … suggests love seems light and pleasant, but is really heavy to bear.

e … shows how powerful he feels his love is.

(1) Draw ✏️ lines to link Shakespeare's language and structure choices to the effect they would have on an audience.

> Try to keep your quotations short so that your comments are very specific.

(2) a Underline Ⓐ any other interesting language or structural choices in the short extract above.

   b Write ✏️ **one** or **two** sentences explaining their effect. Link your comments to the presentation of love or of Romeo.

....
....
....

Unit 3 Commenting on the writer's choices in the extract

Commenting on the writer's choices in the extract

To comment effectively on Shakespeare's choices in the extract, you need to:
- think about the connotations of relevant language choices
- think about the style of speech used and the placement and length of lines
- use short, relevant quotations and comment on their effect.

(For more help on structuring a paragraph of analysis, see Unit 2.)

Look at this exam-style question you saw at the start of the unit on page 17.

Exam-style question

Starting with this extract, how does Shakespeare present romantic love in *Romeo and Juliet*?.

1 Can you identify all the different things the student has included in this paragraph? Link ✏ the annotations to the paragraph to show where the student has included them.

Key features of an effective paragraph of analysis:

- key point focusing on the key words in the question
- evidence from the text to support the point
- comments on the evidence and its impact
- a response to the question

In this extract, romantic love is presented as painful and cruel. First, there is an exchange of several short lines between Benvolio and Romeo where Benvolio finishes Romeo's sentences with questions: 'In love?/Out –/Of love?'. The short, sharp structure of these lines introduces the idea that falling in and out of love can hurt. Benvolio then emphasises this negative side of romantic love by personifying it as something 'gentle' to look at but 'tyrannous' in reality. This suggests that love can be pleasant, as 'gentle' has connotations of kindness and understanding. However, Shakespeare's use of the adjective 'tyrannous' suggests that love is really very harsh and controlling, causing suffering and oppression.

Key features of an effective comment on the writer's choices:

- a comment on language choice(s)
- short quotations as evidence of language choices
- use of subject terminology
- a comment on structural choice(s)

Get back on track

Your turn!

You are now going to **write one or two paragraphs** in response to the exam-style question below, focusing on Extract A on page 18.

Exam-style question

Starting with this extract, how does Shakespeare present romantic love in *Romeo and Juliet*?

Write about:

- how Shakespeare presents romantic love in this extract
- how Shakespeare presents romantic love in the play as a whole.

(30 marks)
AO4 (4 marks)

1. How do you think Shakespeare presents romantic love in this extract (from Romeo: Alas, that Love...)? Write ✏ **one or two** sentences summing up your response.

   ....
   ....
   ....

2. Now look closely at four or five lines from the extract. Select **one** short quotation that clearly supports your answer to question ① above. Underline Ⓐ it on page 18.

3. Think about words or phrases in your chosen section that make a significant contribution to your answer to question ① above.

   a. Which words or phrases reveal something interesting about romantic love? Circle Ⓐ them on page 18.

   b. What are the connotations of those words and phrases? What do they suggest about romantic love? Annotate ✏ them.

4. Now think about Shakespeare's structural choices in your chosen section. Think about:

   - the line's position in the scene
   - the length of the line(s)
   - the style of speech used in the line(s).

   Do Shakespeare's structural choices in your chosen section make a significant contribution to your answer to question ① above? How? Annotate ✏ your chosen section with your ideas.

5. Using all the ideas you have noted, write ✏ **one** paragraph in response to the exam-style question above.

   ....
   ....
   ....
   ....

6. Repeat questions ②–⑤, focusing on a different section of the extract. ✏

Unit 3 Commenting on the writer's choices in the extract   23

Review your skills

Check up

Review your response to the exam-style question on page 23. Tick ✓ the column to show how well you think you have done each of the following.

	Not quite ✓	Nearly there ✓	Got it! ✓
structured an effective paragraph of analysis in response to the question	☐	☐	☐
commented on Shakespeare's language choices	☐	☐	☐
commented on Shakespeare's structural choices	☐	☐	☐

Need more practice?

Here is another exam-style question, this time relating to the extract from Act 3 Scene 5 on page 74 (Extract B).

> **Exam-style question**
>
> Starting with this extract, explore how Shakespeare presents the Nurse in *Romeo and Juliet*.
>
> Write about:
> - how Shakespeare presents the Nurse in this extract
> - how Shakespeare presents the Nurse in the play as a whole.
>
> (30 marks)
>
> AO4 (4 marks)

Write ✏ **one** or **two** paragraphs in response to this question, focusing on language and structure **in the extract only**.

You'll find some suggested ideas in the Answers section.

How confident do you feel about each of these **skills?** Colour ✏ in the bars.

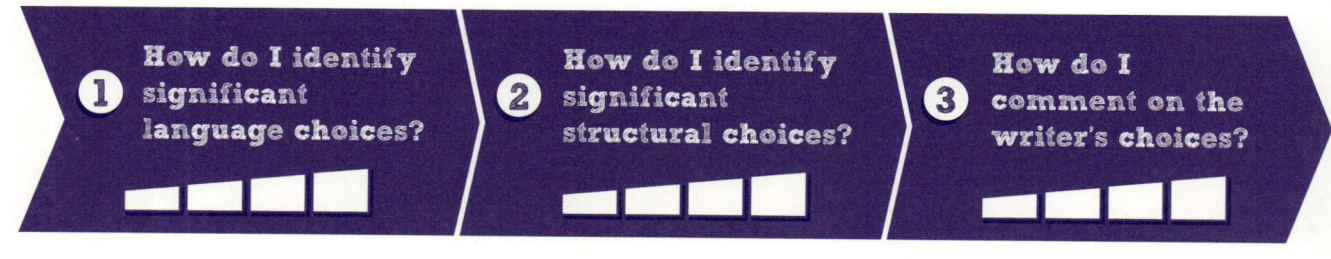

1. How do I identify significant language choices?
2. How do I identify significant structural choices?
3. How do I comment on the writer's choices?

Get started — Read, understand and respond to texts (AO1)

④ Exploring themes and characters

This unit will help you to explore how the characters and themes of *Romeo and Juliet* develop in the play, and help you to develop your response to them. The skills you will build are to:

- track how characters develop in the play
- track how themes develop in the play
- comment on the development of characters and themes in the play.

In the exam you will face questions like the one below. This is about the extract on the next page. At the end of the unit you will **plan and write one or two paragraphs** in response to this question.

> **Exam-style question**
>
> Starting with this extract, explain how far you think Shakespeare presents Juliet as disobedient.
>
> Write about:
> - how Shakespeare presents Juliet as disobedient in this extract
> - how Shakespeare presents Juliet as disobedient in the play as a whole.
>
> (30 marks)
> AO4 (4 marks)

Before you tackle the question you will work through three key questions in the **skills boosts** to help you explore the play's themes and characters.

① How do I track the development of a character?

② How do I track the development of a theme?

③ How do I comment on the development of character or theme?

Read the extract on the next page from Act 3 Scene 2 of *Romeo and Juliet*.

As you read, think about the following:

- What has happened before this scene? What happens after this scene?
- How does Shakespeare present Juliet in this extract?
- How is loyalty presented in this extract?

Unit 4 Exploring themes and characters

Get started

Exam-style question

Read the following extract from Act 3 Scene 2 of *Romeo and Juliet*.

At this point in the play Juliet has just heard about Tybalt's death and is finding it hard to believe that it was Romeo who killed her cousin.

Extract A | Act 3 Scene 2 of *Romeo and Juliet*

JULIET
O serpent heart, hid with a flowering face!
Did ever dragon keep so fair a cave?
Beautiful tyrant! fiend angelical! –
Dove-feathered raven, wolvish-ravening lamb! –
5   Despisèd substance of divinest show –
Just opposite to what thou justly seem'st,
A damnèd saint, an honourable villain!
O nature, what hadst thou to do in hell
When thou didst bower the spirit of a fiend
10 In mortal paradise of such sweet flesh?
Was ever book containing such vile matter
So fairly bound? O, that deceit should dwell
In such a gorgeous palace!
NURSE
There's no trust,
15 No faith, no honesty in men. – All perjured,
All forsworn, all naught, all dissemblers!
Ah, where's my man? Give me some aqua-vitae.
These griefs, these woes, these sorrows make me old.
Shame come to Romeo!
JULIET
20 Blistered be thy tongue
For such a wish! He was not born to shame!
Upon his brow shame is ashamed to sit,
For 'tis a throne where honour may be crowned
Sole monarch of the universal earth.
25 O, what a beast was I to chide at him!
NURSE
Will you speak well of him that killed your cousin?
JULIET
Shall I speak ill of him that is my husband?
Ah, poor my lord, what tongue shall smooth thy name,
When I, thy three-hours' wife, have mangled it?
30 But wherefore, villain, didst thou kill my cousin?
That villain cousin would have killed my husband.
Back, foolish tears, back to your native spring –
Your tributary drops belong to woe,
Which you, mistaking, offer up to joy.

Unit 4 Exploring themes and characters

Skills boost

1 How do I track the development of a character?

The key characters in the play are Romeo and Juliet. To write effectively about them in the play as a whole, you need to think about how Shakespeare's presentation of them changes as the action of the play develops.

1 Think about how Romeo and Juliet are presented at the **start** of the play in Acts 1 and 2.

1.2	Romeo is infatuated with Rosaline	1.2	Juliet's father tells Paris she is too young to marry
1.4	Romeo is miserable on the way to the Capulets' ball	1.3	Juliet has little interest in love or marriage
1.5	Romeo falls in love with Juliet at first sight	2.2	Juliet declares her love for Romeo from her balcony
2.1	Romeo lingers in Juliet's garden	2.2	Juliet suggests they marry the following day

How would you sum up the characters of Romeo and Juliet at the start of the play? Write R or J beneath any of the words below and/or add your own ideas.

| romantic | immature | innocent | foolish | impulsive | depressed | obedient | |

2 Now look at some of the key scenes showing the development of the characters of Romeo and Juliet.

3.1	Romeo refuses to fight Tybalt.	/5	2.6	Juliet marries Romeo in secret.	/5
3.1	Romeo kills Tybalt to avenge Mercutio's death.	/5	3.2	Juliet learns of Tybalt's death but defends Romeo.	/5
3.3	Romeo asks Friar Lawrence for advice.	/5	3.5	Juliet refuses to marry Paris.	/5
5.1	Romeo hears Juliet has died.	/5	4.3	Juliet drinks the potion.	/5

a How significant is each of these scenes in the development of each character from the start to the end of the play? Give each one a mark out of five: 1/5 = not at all significant; 5/5 = highly significant.

b Write one or two sentences summing up how the characters of Romeo and Juliet develop and change during the course of the play.

....

....

Unit 4 Exploring themes and characters   27

Skills boost

2 How do I track the development of a theme?

> To track the way in which Shakespeare explores a theme of the play, you need to identify key scenes in which that theme is featured and think about the ideas it raises for the audience.

1 Look at some of the **key themes** and **key events** in *Romeo and Juliet* below.

- A love
- B revenge
- C disobedience
- D conflict
- E loyalty
- F fate
- G family

- a **1.1** The servants meet in the street
- b **3.1** Romeo fights with, and kills, Tybalt
- c **1.3** Juliet's mother urges her to marry Paris
- d **5.1** Friar Lawrence's letter does not reach Romeo
- e **3.5** Lord Capulet threatens to disown Juliet
- f **1.1** Lord Montague worries about Romeo's mood
- g **1.5** Tybalt is angry that Romeo is at his family's party

   a. Draw ✏️ lines to match each theme to an event. ==Some events may match more than one theme.==

   b. Select and highlight ✏️ **one** key event. Annotate ✏️ the text above with your ideas about how it links to **one** of the themes.

2 A **key theme** is an idea that Shakespeare explores in different ways at different points in the play. Look at some of the key scenes in which Shakespeare explores the theme of **conflict**.

- **1.1** Gregory and Sampson exchange insults with the Montague servants.
- **1.1** Prince Escalus threatens to execute anybody found fighting.
- **1.5** Lord Capulet argues with Tybalt about Romeo being at the ball.
- **3.1** Mercutio is killed by a blow under Romeo's arm.
- **3.5** Juliet refuses to marry Paris.
- **5.3** Romeo and Paris fight at Juliet's tomb.

   a. How does Shakespeare develop ideas about conflict? Add ✏️ the ideas below to the events.

comic	verbal	➤	dramatic	violent	➤	tragic	family
light-hearted	bawdy		foolhardy	dangerous		moving	deadly
entertaining	slapstick		honourable	loyal		serious	final

   b. Use your answers from a to write ✏️ **one** or **two** sentences explaining your ideas on paper.

Unit 4 Exploring themes and characters

Skills boost

3 How do I comment on the development of character or theme?

One way to explore how characters develop is to **compare** how they are presented at the start and end of the play; one way to explore how themes develop is to **compare** how they are presented in different key scenes in the play.

1 Look at these key moments in the development of the character of Juliet.

> When we are first introduced to Juliet in Act 1 Scene 3, she is with her nurse and shows no interest in love or getting married, but does agree to think about marrying Paris. This presents her as both .... and ....
> When she meets Romeo in Act 1 Scene 5, she encourages his romantic attention. This presents her as ....
> Then, in Act 2 Scene 2, she is presented as becoming more .... when she suggests marrying Romeo in secret the next day.
> Later in the play, when ....
> she is shown as ....

a Complete 🖉 the notes above, summing up how Juliet changes during the course of the play.

b How is Juliet presented in the final act of the play when she wakes from the potion-induced sleep? Write 🖉 **one** or **two** sentences summing up your ideas.

....
....

2 Look at these key moments in the play at which the theme of loyalty is shown.

- A `1.1` Sampson and Gregory threaten the Montague servants.
- B `1.1` Benvolio tries to help Lady Montague find out what is wrong with Romeo.
- C `3.1` Romeo avenges the death of Mercutio.   D `3.5` Juliet forgives Romeo for killing Tybalt.
- E `3.5` Juliet feels betrayed when the Nurse suggests she marry Paris.

a Look at the statements below about loyalty. Write 🖉 the letter of the scene above next to the statement the scene matches best.

i	Loyalty is foolish, as it leads to violence and death.	☐	iii	Loyalty is very important.	☐
ii	Family loyalty extends even to the lowest in status.	☐	iv	A betrayal of loyalty can break even the strongest ties between people.	☐

b Write 🖉 **one** or **two** sentences on paper summing up your view of the different ways loyalty is presented in *Romeo and Juliet*.

> When thinking about a theme, always consider how far it contributes to the deaths of Romeo and Juliet.

Unit 4 Exploring themes and characters

Get back on track

Exploring themes and characters

To explore the themes and characters in *Romeo and Juliet* effectively, you need to:
- identify significant key events in the play in which those characters or themes are shown
- compare how they are presented in those key events.

Look at this exam-style question you saw at the start of the unit.

> **Exam-style question**
>
> Starting with this extract, explain how far you think Shakespeare presents Juliet as disobedient.
>
> Write about:
> - how Shakespeare presents Juliet as disobedient in this extract
> - how Shakespeare presents Juliet as disobedient in the play as a whole.

1 Now look at these two paragraphs, written by a student in response to the exam-style question above.

> Juliet is first presented to the audience through her father, who tells Paris that she is too young to marry at only fourteen. Juliet then appears, accompanied by first her nurse and then her nurse and her mother, which emphasises her youth and immaturity. Shakespeare presents her as innocent and child-like as she has no interest in marriage, declaring it an 'honour that I dream not of'.
>
> At this point she is not presented as disobedient, as she agrees to consider Paris as a suitor, and even says she will not go further than her mother would approve of.
>
> However, Juliet is soon shown to be more independent than these early scenes suggest.
>
> Although Romeo starts their relationship, Juliet does encourage him by responding to his kiss at her family's ball and she is presented as knowing her own mind as she declares her love for him in the balcony scene. This suggests she is becoming rebellious as she knows that he is an enemy of her family.

a Circle (A) and label (✏) **all** the key scenes or events in the play that this student has referred to in these paragraphs.

b Underline (A) and label (✏) where in these paragraphs this student **comments** on how Shakespeare presents Juliet's attitude in these key scenes or events.

c Highlight (✏) and label (✏) where in these paragraphs this student has shown an understanding of the **development** of Juliet's character.

Unit 4 Exploring themes and characters

Get back on track

Your turn!

You are now going to **write two paragraphs** in response to the exam-style question.

> **Exam-style question**
>
> Starting with this extract, explain how far you think Shakespeare presents Juliet as disobedient.
>
> Write about:
> - how Shakespeare presents Juliet as disobedient in this extract
> - how Shakespeare presents Juliet as disobedient in the play as a whole.
>
> (30 marks)
> AO4 (4 marks)

1 Which key scenes or events in the play could you focus on in your response? Note ✎ **four** of your ideas below.

Think about:

> ❓ When and how is Juliet presented as disobedient?

> ❓ How does Juliet change over the course of the play?

1

2

3

4

2 Look carefully at the key scenes or events you have chosen. What do they suggest about how Juliet's attitude is presented in the play? Add ✎ to your notes.

3 Now consider how Juliet is presented in the extract on page 26. How far is she presented as disobedient in this scene? Add ✎ to your notes.

4 Use your notes above to write ✎ **two** paragraphs on paper in response to the exam-style question.

Unit 4 Exploring themes and characters   **31**

Review your skills

Check up

Review your response to the exam-style question on page 31. Tick ✓ the column to show how well you think you have done each of the following.

	Not quite ✓	Nearly there ✓	Got it! ✓
identified significant scenes or events in the play showing Juliet's character	☐	☐	☐
commented on how Juliet's character is presented in each significant scene or event	☐	☐	☐
commented on how Juliet's character changes during the course of the play	☐	☐	☐

Need more practice?

Here is another exam-style question, this time relating to the extract from Act 3 Scene 5 on page 74 (Extract B).

Exam-style question

Starting with this extract, explore how Shakespeare presents the Nurse in *Romeo and Juliet*.

Write about:
- how Shakespeare presents the Nurse in this extract
- how Shakespeare presents the Nurse in the play as a whole.

(30 marks)
AO4 (4 marks)

Write ✏️ two paragraphs in response to this question, focusing on the second bullet point: **the play as a whole**.

You'll find some suggested ideas in the Answers section.

How confident do you feel about each of these **skills**? Colour ✏️ in the bars.

1. How do I track the development of a character?
2. How do I track the development of a theme?
3. How do I comment on the development of character or theme?

Unit 4 Exploring themes and characters

Get started Read, understand and respond to texts (AO1)

⑤ Planning your response

This unit will help you to plan your response to the exam question. The skills you will build are to:

- develop a critical judgement in response to the focus of the exam question
- support your judgement with relevant points
- sequence your points to build a successful argument in support of your judgement.

In the exam you will face a question like the one below. This is about the extract on the next page. At the end of the unit you will **write your own response** to this question.

Exam-style question

Starting with this extract, explore how Shakespeare presents revenge in *Romeo and Juliet*.

Write about:
- how Shakespeare presents revenge in this extract
- how Shakespeare presents revenge in the play as a whole.

(30 marks)
AO4 (4 marks)

Before you tackle the question you will work through three key questions in the **skills boosts** to help you plan your response.

① How do I make a critical judgement? ② How do I gather relevant points? ③ How do I sequence my points?

Read the extract on the next page from Act 3 Scene 1 of *Romeo and Juliet*.

As you read, think about the following:

- What has happened before this scene? What happens after this scene?
- How does Shakespeare present ideas about revenge in this scene?
- How does Shakespeare present Romeo in this scene?

Exam-style question

Read the following extract from Act 3 Scene 1 of *Romeo and Juliet*.

At this point in the play Mercutio has just been fatally wounded during a fight with Tybalt and blamed the feud between the Capulets and the Montagues before being taken away by Benvolio.

Extract A | Act 3 Scene 1 of *Romeo and Juliet*

ROMEO
This gentleman, the Prince's near ally,
My very friend, hath got this mortal hurt
In *my* behalf: my reputation stained
With Tybalt's slander. – Tybalt! – that an hour
5 Hath been my cousin! O sweet Juliet –
Thy beauty hath made me effeminate
And in my temper softened valour's steel!
Re-enter BENVOLIO.
BENVOLIO
O Romeo, Romeo! Brave Mercutio is dead!
That gallant spirit hath aspired the clouds,
10 Which too untimely here did scorn the earth.
ROMEO
This day's black fate on more days doth depend:
This but begins the woe others must end.
Re-enter TYBALT.
BENVOLIO
Here comes the furious Tybalt back again.
ROMEO
Alive – in triumph! And Mercutio slain!
15 Away to heaven respective lenity,
And fire-eyed fury be my conduct now!
Now, Tybalt, take the 'villain' back again
That late thou gavest me – for Mercutio's soul
Is but a little way above our heads,
20 Staying for thine to keep him company.
Either thou or I, or both, must go with him.
TYBALT
Thou, wretched boy, that didst consort him here,
Shalt with him hence!
ROMEO
(Drawing his sword) This shall determine that.
They fight. ROMEO kills TYBALT.
BENVOLIO
25 Romeo, away, be gone!
The citizens are up, and Tybalt slain.
Stand not amazed! The Prince will doom thee death
If thou art taken. Hence, be gone, away!
ROMEO
O, I am fortune's fool!

Skills boost

1 How do I make a critical judgement?

Before you plan your written response, you need to make a **critical judgement** on the topic in the question. This means weighing up the key evidence in the play and coming to a conclusion: a sentence or two that sums up your ideas.

1 One way to begin developing your critical judgement is to focus on the extract you are given in the question. Look at two quotations from Extract A on page 34.

Romeo

> Away to heaven respective lenity,
> And fire-eyed fury be my conduct now!

Benvolio

> Stand not amazed! The Prince will doom thee death
> If thou art taken. Hence, be gone, away!

a How do Romeo and Benvolio feel about revenge?
Note your ideas in the boxes above. Use some of the words below, or add your own.

| honourable | necessary | foolish | dangerous | justified |

b Write one or two sentences summing up your **critical judgement** on how revenge is presented **in the extract**.

....

2 Now you need to think about how revenge is explored **in the play as a whole**. Look at these other scenes that show characters affected by revenge.

| 1.1 | The Prince warns about any further public fighting. | | 3.1 | Tybalt is killed by Romeo. | | 5.3 | Romeo kills himself. | |

a Which of these scenes could be used as evidence to **support** or **develop** the critical judgement that you made in 1 b? Tick ✓ them.

b Which of these scenes **contradict** the critical judgement that you made? Cross ✗ them.

c Is your critical judgement on how Shakespeare explores revenge in *Romeo and Juliet* still valid? Or do you need to rethink it now that you have considered some of the other scenes in which revenge is shown? Either tick ✓ your answer to 1 b, or rewrite it below.

....
....

Unit 5 Planning your response

Skills boost

2 How do I gather relevant points?

You need to gather a range of points from the extract and from the whole play to support and develop the critical judgement you make in response to the exam question.

1 Think about how revenge is presented **in the extract** on page 34 and **in the whole play**.

a Look at some different critical judgements about the presentation of revenge in *Romeo and Juliet* below. For each one, circle (A) the number on the scale to show how strongly you agree or disagree.

	Disagree	Unsure	Agree
A Revenge is related to family honour.	1	2	3
B Revenge can be very destructive.	1	2	3
C Revenge ultimately leads to tragedy.	1	2	3
D The audience expects revenge to be a key factor from the start.	1	2	3
E Characters who seek revenge believe they are driven by fate.	1	2	3

b Now look at some of the key scenes from the play below. Select key scenes that support each of the judgements that you agreed with, labelling them **A, B, C**, etc. to show which judgement they support.

- **Prologue** The play will end in tragedy because of the feud.
- **1.1** The Capulet servants taunt the Montague servants.
- **3.1** Mercutio is killed by Tybalt.
- **3.1** Romeo is banished after killing Tybalt.
- **5.3** Romeo and Juliet kill themselves.
- **3.5** Juliet's loyalties are torn between her love for Romeo and her grief for Tybalt.
- **5.3** Lord Capulet asks Lord Montague to join him in ending the feud.

2 a Review all of your answers on this page so far. Use them to note down in the table **three** key points you might make in your response to the exam-style question.

b For each key point, note the key scenes from the play that you could refer to as **evidence** to support your point.

	Key point	Evidence
1		
2		
3		

Unit 5 Planning your response

Skills boost

3 How do I sequence my points?

You need to sequence your key points to build a logical argument that supports your critical judgement. You need to start with the extract – but where do you go from there?

Look at this exam-style question, and one student's critical judgement in response to it.

Exam-style question

Starting with this extract, explore how Shakespeare presents revenge in *Romeo and Juliet*.

> In 'Romeo and Juliet', Shakespeare presents revenge as linked to the families' feud. It becomes more and more dangerous as the play progresses and contributes significantly to the deaths of Romeo and Juliet.

Now look at these four key points, taken from the same student's plan.

A Revenge is dangerous – Tybalt wants revenge for Mercutio's insults/both are killed.

B Revenge is sometimes avoided – Lord Capulet stops Tybalt ejecting Romeo from the ball.

C Revenge is shown to be foolish – Romeo realises his own folly after he is banished.

D Revenge leads to tragedy – Juliet finds Romeo dead and kills herself.

(1) One way to sequence the key points in a response is to work your way through the play **chronologically**: exploring how a character or theme develops as the play progresses.

How would you sequence the four key points above if you were organising this response **chronologically**? Write ✏ the letters A–D in the order in which you would sequence them.

☐ ☐ ☐ ☐

(2) Another way to organise the key points in a response is to **synthesise** your key points: grouping related points together.

For example, you could:

chronological: in time order
synthesise: combine or group together

(a) group your key points by **character**. ☐

How would you sequence the key points above if you were going to explore how Shakespeare shows revenge first in one **character** and then another? Write ✏ the letters A–D.

☐ ☐ ☐ ☐

Or you could:

(b) group your key points by **approach**. ☐

How would you sequence the key points above if you were going to look at one way in which Shakespeare explores revenge, and then another way in which Shakespeare explores revenge? ✏

☐ ☐ ☐ ☐

(3) Look at all of your answers above. Which method would **you** choose to sequence the key points above? Tick ✓ it.

Unit 5 Planning your response

Planning your response

Get back on track

To plan an effective response, you need to:
- make a critical judgement summing up your response to the focus of the question
- gather relevant points: identify the key moments in the play that support your critical judgement and use them to develop points you can make in your response
- sequence your points: decide on the most effective way to build a logical argument that supports your critical judgement: for example, chronologically, or by character, or by approach.

Look at this exam-style question you saw at the start of the unit.

Exam-style question

Starting with this extract, explore how Shakespeare presents revenge in *Romeo and Juliet*.

Write about:
- how Shakespeare presents revenge in this extract
- how Shakespeare presents revenge in the play as a whole.

1 Now look at these two paragraphs, written by a student in response to the exam-style question above.

> In the opening scene of 'Romeo and Juliet', the Capulet servants taunt the Montague servants when they arrive in the square. At this point, Shakespeare suggests that not all the characters are going to be fuelled by revenge as Benvolio tries to stop the fighting, but Tybalt arrives and immediately wants revenge for insults against his family. After the fight, the Prince declares that any future fighting will result in execution, which forewarns the audience of the importance revenge will have later in the play.
>
> In Act 3 Scene 1, the audience sees how destructive revenge can be when Mercutio gets angry at Romeo's refusal to respond to Tybalt's insults. The mood of the scene goes from comic, with Mercutio relaxed and making jokes, to heated and dangerous when Mercutio calls Romeo's lack of response a 'vile submission'. Mercutio's death suggests revenge is both dangerous and foolish, as he is killed accidentally, under the arm of Romeo.

a Which of these critical judgements do these paragraphs support? Tick ✓ **one, or more**.

A	Shakespeare shows the destructive force of revenge by presenting it as becoming more and more dangerous.	☐
B	Shakespeare uses ideas about revenge to manipulate the audience's feelings about particular characters.	☐
C	Shakespeare links ideas about revenge to the families' feud and presents it as increasingly destructive.	☐

b How has this student organised their key points? Tick ✓ **one**.

A	chronologically	☐
B	by character	☐
C	by approach	☐

Get back on track

Your turn!

You are now going to **write your own answer** in response to the exam-style question.

> **Exam-style question**
>
> Starting with this extract, explore how Shakespeare presents revenge in *Romeo and Juliet*.
>
> Write about:
> - how Shakespeare presents revenge in this extract
> - how Shakespeare presents revenge in the play as a whole.
>
> (30 marks)
> AO4 (4 marks)

1. Sum up your **critical judgement** in response to the exam-style question above. This will be the **conclusion** that your response must support.

   ....
   ....
   ....

2. Which **key events or scenes** in the play will you explore in your response to support your critical judgement? Note them below.

   [ ]

3. Note down all the **key points** you will make about these key events or scenes to support your critical judgement.

   ....
   ....
   ....

4. a. How will you sequence your key points? Tick ✓ **one** answer.

   chronologically [ ]   by character [ ]   by approach [ ]

   b. Number your key points in ③, sequencing them to build an argument that supports your critical judgement.

5. Now write your response to the exam-style question above on paper.

Unit 5 Planning your response

Review your skills

Check up

Review your response to the exam-style question on page 39. Tick ✓ the column to show how well you think you have done each of the following.

	Not quite ✓	Nearly there ✓	Got it! ✓
made a critical judgement	☐	☐	☐
made key points using key scenes and events in the play to support my critical judgement	☐	☐	☐
sequenced my key points to build an argument that supports my critical judgement	☐	☐	☐

Look over all of your work in this unit. Note ✎ down the **three** most important things to remember when planning your response.

1. ....
2. ....
3. ....

Need more practice?

Here is another exam-style question, this time relating to the extract from Act 2 Scene 3 on page 75 (Extract C).

Exam-style question

Starting with this extract, explore how Shakespeare presents Friar Lawrence in *Romeo and Juliet*.

Write about:
- how Shakespeare presents Friar Lawrence in this extract
- how Shakespeare presents Friar Lawrence in the play as a whole.

(30 marks)
AO4 (4 marks)

Plan ✎ your response to this question. Aim to:
- sum up your critical judgement in one or two sentences
- identify key events to focus on, and key points to make
- sequence your ideas.

You'll find some suggested ideas in the Answers section.

How confident do you feel about each of these **skills?** Colour ✎ in the bars.

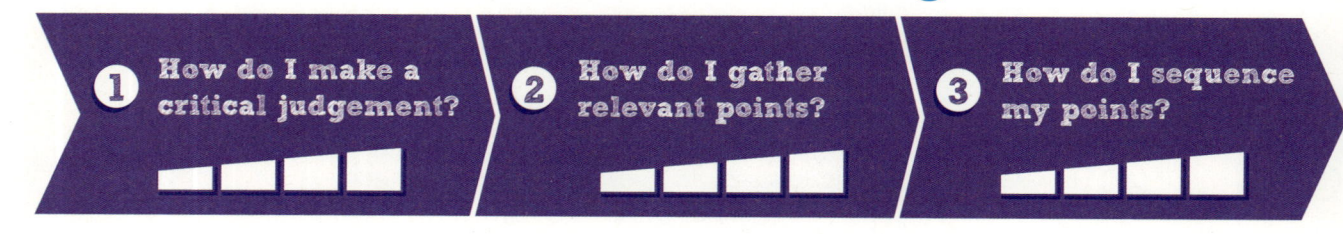

1 How do I make a critical judgement?

2 How do I gather relevant points?

3 How do I sequence my points?

Get started

Read, understand and respond to texts (AO1); Analyse the language, form and structure used by a writer to create meanings and effects (AO2)

⑥ Writing your response

This unit will help you write the part of your response in which you have to focus on **the play as a whole**. The skills you will build are to:

- know key events and key quotations you can use when writing about the play as a whole
- understand how to use key events and quotations as evidence
- be able to analyse evidence from the play effectively.

In the exam you will face a question like the one below. This is about the extract on the next page. At the end of the unit you will **write your own response** to the **second part** of this question.

Reminder: For more help on writing about **the extract**, see Units 2 and 3.

> **Exam-style question**
>
> Starting with this extract, explore how Shakespeare presents parent–child relationships in *Romeo and Juliet*.
>
> Write about:
> - how Shakespeare presents parent–child relationships at this moment in the play
> - how Shakespeare presents parent–child relationships in the play as a whole.
>
> (30 marks)
> AO4 (4 marks)

Before you tackle the question you will work through three key questions in the **skills boosts** to help you write your response.

① How do I choose key events and key quotations to learn?
② How do I use evidence to support my ideas?
③ How do I analyse my evidence?

Read the extract on the next page from Act 3 Scene 5 of *Romeo and Juliet*.

As you read, think about the following:

- What has happened before this scene? What happens after this scene?
- How does Shakespeare present the relationship between Lady Capulet and Juliet?
- How does Shakespeare present Lady Capulet in this extract?

Unit 6 Writing your response 41

Get started

> **Exam-style question**
>
> Read the following extract from Act 3 Scene 5 of *Romeo and Juliet*.
>
> At this point in the play, Juliet has just found out that Romeo killed her cousin Tybalt but has decided to forgive him despite her grief. Her mother then tells Juliet to prepare to marry Paris in two days' time.

Extract A | Act 3 Scene 5 of *Romeo and Juliet*

LADY CAPULET
Well, well, thou hast a careful father, child –
One who, to put thee from thy heaviness,
Hath sorted out a sudden day of joy
That thou expects not, nor I looked not for.
JULIET
5 Madam, in happy time! What day is that?
LADY CAPULET
Marry, my child, early next Thursday morn,
The gallant, young and noble gentleman,
The County Paris, at Saint Peter's Church,
Shall happily make thee there a joyful bride.
JULIET
10 Now, by Saint Peter's Church, and Peter too,
He shall *not* make me there a joyful bride!
I wonder at this haste, that I must wed
Ere he that should be husband comes to woo!
I pray you tell my lord and father, madam,
15 I will not marry yet. And when I do, I swear
It shall be Romeo, whom you know I hate,
Rather than Paris. These are news indeed!
LADY CAPULET
Here comes your father. Tell him so yourself,
And see how he will take it at your hands.

Skills boost

1 How do I choose key events and key quotations to learn?

When you write about the **extract**, you should support your response with quotations from the extract. When you write about the **play as a whole**, you should refer to key events and scenes. You can also use some key quotations that you have learned to show your detailed understanding of the play.

Reminder: For more help on writing about the **extract**, see Units 2 and 3.

The key events in the play are those that: show a significant aspect of a key character **or** explore a key theme **or** are significant to the plot – the play would not develop in the same way without them.

1 Look at the extract from Act 3 Scene 5 on page 42 (Extract A). Add ✏ words from the selection below to these sentences to explain the significance of this moment in the play.

a. At this point Lady Capulet is shown to be a .... parent.

b. .... ideas about parental love are shown at this point in the play.

| caring | loving | distant | harsh | interesting | important |

2 Now look at some of the other events in Act 3, the middle of the play.

3.1	Romeo refuses to fight Tybalt.
3.1	Mercutio curses both families after he is stabbed by Tybalt.
3.2	Juliet is horrified at Tybalt's death, but decides to forgive Romeo.
3.3	Friar Lawrence advises Romeo and agrees to help him.
3.5	Lord Capulet threatens to disown Juliet when she refuses to marry Paris

a. Which scenes reveal something about key characters? Highlight ✏ those characters' names.

b. Which explore a key theme? Label ✏ them with the theme they reveal.

c. Review your answers to questions ① and ②. Which key scenes and events in Act 3 should you make sure you know? Tick ✓ them.

3 The best quotations to learn are short, and can be used to support two (or more) different ideas. Look at some of Juliet's lines from Act 2 Scene 2.

A. O Romeo, Romeo! Wherefore art thou Romeo? Deny thy father and refuse thy name –

B. What's in a name? That which we call a rose By any other word would smell as sweet.

C. And all my fortunes at thy foot I'll lay, And follow thee, my lord, throughout the world.

D. Good night, good night. Parting is such sweet sorrow,

a. Which quotations most effectively show the difficulty for Juliet of her love for Romeo? Tick ✓ **at least two**.

b. All the quotations show something about love, but which one also reveals something about another key theme? Label ✏ it with the theme.

c. Look at the quotations you have chosen. How could you make them shorter and easier to remember? Underline Ⓐ the most significant or revealing phrase of two to four words in each.

Unit 6 Writing your response 43

Skills boost

2 How do I use evidence to support my ideas?

You can use **key events** in the play and **key quotations** as evidence to **support** and **explain** your ideas.

Look at one student's **key idea**, or **critical judgement**, in response to this exam question.

Exam-style question
Starting with this extract, explore how Shakespeare presents parent–child relationships in *Romeo and Juliet*.

> Parent–child relationships in Romeo and Juliet are presented as difficult.

(1) Look again at Extract A on page 42. Note down **one key event** and **one key quotation** from this point in the play to support the student's **key idea**.

Key event: ....

Key quotation: ....

(2) Now think about **key events** elsewhere in the play. Which would support the key idea above?

Note down **two** key events.

Hint: Think about both Juliet and Romeo when considering relationships.

1 ....   2 ....

(3) Which **key quotations** from the play would support the key idea above? Tick ✓ the **four** most effective quotations.

A 1.1 Lord Montague says of Romeo *But to himself so secret and so close,* ☐	**B** 1.2 Lord Capulet says to Paris about Juliet *She is the hopeful lady of my earth.* ☐
C 1.3 The Nurse says to Juliet *thou wast the prettiest babe that e'er I nursed.* ☐	**D** 1.3 Lady Capulet says to Juliet *Read o'er the volume of young Paris' face, And find delight writ there with beauty's pen.* ☐
E 3.5 Lady Capulet says of Juliet *I would the fool were married to her grave!* ☐	**F** 3.5 Lord Capulet says to Juliet *Hang thee, young baggage! Disobedient wretch!* ☐
G 3.5 Lord Capulet says to his wife *My fingers itch.* ☐	**H** 5.3 Lord Montague says at the tomb *Alas, my liege, my wife is dead tonight. Grief of my son's exile hath stopped her breath.* ☐

(4) Review the evidence you have gathered above. Which supports the key idea at the top of this page most effectively? ✓

☐ The key events you noted in **(2)**?   ☐ The quotations you selected in **(3)**?   ☐ or both?

44   Unit 6 Writing your response

Skills boost

3 How do I analyse my evidence?

Every key **idea or point** you make should be supported with **evidence** that you can **analyse**, exploring the effect of the writer's choices of language and structure, what it suggests about theme and character, and its impact on the audience.

Look at one student's key idea, or **critical judgement**, on the theme of parent–child relationships in *Romeo and Juliet*.

> At several points in the play, parent–child relationships are presented as caring.

Now look at a **key quotation** you could use as evidence to support this key idea.

> Before the ball, Lord Capulet tells Paris to 'But woo her, gentle Paris, get her heart'.

To develop an effective analysis, think about these **five areas** of analysis:

A — **Explain the quote in the context of the play:** Why does Lord Capulet say this?
> Paris has asked for Juliet's hand in marriage but Lord Capulet thinks she is too young at fourteen.

B — **Think about language and structure:** What do 'woo her' and 'get her heart' suggest?
> They suggest he wants Paris to treat Juliet with kindness and gain her love before he will agree to the marriage.

C — **Think about character:** What does this suggest about Lord Capulet's character?
> He cares about Juliet as he obviously wants her to marry for love.

D — **Think about theme:** What does this suggest about parent–child relationships?
> It presents the relationship between Juliet and her father as close: he cares about her future happiness.

E — **Think about Shakespeare's intention:** How does Shakespeare want the audience to respond to Lord Capulet at this point in the play?
>

① **a** Look at one student's ideas for analysis of the **key quotation** above. Which ideas would you include in your own analysis of this quote? Tick ✓ them.

   b Complete ✏ the final analysis point with your ideas about audience response.

② Now look at a key event that you could use as evidence to support the key idea above.

> In Act 1, Lord Montague asks Benvolio to find out what is wrong with Romeo.

Use the **five areas of analysis** above to help you note ✏ some ideas you could use in your analysis of this key event. Continue on paper.

Unit 6 Writing your response

Writing your response

Get back on track

To write an effective response, you should:
- be familiar with the key events of the play
- know some key quotations from the play off by heart
- use key events and key quotations as evidence to support your ideas about the play's key themes and characters
- analyse your evidence, thinking about language, structure, theme, character and Shakespeare's intention.

Look at this exam-style question you saw on page 41.

Exam-style question

Starting with this extract, explore how Shakespeare presents parent–child relationships in *Romeo and Juliet*.

Write about:
- how Shakespeare presents parent–child relationships at this moment in the play
- how Shakespeare presents parent–child relationships in the play as a whole.

Now look at a paragraph focusing on the play as a whole, taken from one student's response to the question.

> When Juliet refuses to marry Paris after the death of Tybalt, Lord Capulet shows himself to be a harsh and domineering parent. Before storming off in a rage, he calls her a 'young baggage' and tells her to 'hang, beg, starve, die in the streets' and then talks of disowning her completely. The word 'baggage' suggests she is just an unwanted possession rather than his daughter and the use of harsh verbs such as 'beg' and 'starve' shows the strength of his feelings. At this point, Shakespeare is showing a complete breakdown in parent–child relations that makes Lord Capulet seem to be the villain. This would make the audience start to hate him.

- uses a key event as evidence
- uses a quotation as evidence
- explains the context of the evidence
- analysis comment on the writer's choices of language and/or structure
- analysis comment on character
- analysis comment on theme
- analysis comment on Shakespeare's intention

1 Can you identify all the different things the student has included in this paragraph? Link ✏️ the annotations to the paragraph to show where the student has included them.

Unit 6 Writing your response

Get back on track

Your turn!

You are now going to **write your own answer** in response to the exam-style question.

> **Exam-style question**
>
> Starting with this extract, explore how Shakespeare presents parent–child relationships in *Romeo and Juliet*.
>
> Write about:
> - how Shakespeare presents parent–child relationships at this moment in the play
> - how Shakespeare presents parent–child relationships in the play as a whole.
>
> (30 marks)
>
> AO4 (4 marks)

1. Write ✎ **one** or **two** sentences summarising your critical judgement in response to the question: How are parent–child relationships presented?

   > Remember to think about both Juliet and Romeo when considering parent–child relationships.

   ....

   ....

2. Which key events in the play would support your critical judgement? Note ✎ them below.

   [   ]

3. Which quotations could you explore in your response? Add ✎ them above.

4. Look at all the evidence you have gathered. Think about:
   - language and structure in your quotations
   - what your evidence suggests about the characters
   - what your evidence suggests about the theme of parent–child relations
   - what your evidence suggests about Shakespeare's intention: how might the audience respond at this point?

   Annotate ✎ your evidence with your ideas.

5. Look at your annotated evidence.

   a. Which are your strongest ideas? Tick ✓ them.

   b. Number ✎ the ideas that you have ticked, sequencing them to build an argument that supports your critical judgement.

6. Now write ✎ your response to the exam-style question above on paper.

Unit 6 Writing your response

Review your skills

Check up

Review your response to the exam-style question on page 47. Tick ✓ the column to show how well you think you have done each of the following.

	Not quite ✓	Nearly there ✓	Got it! ✓
selected relevant key events to support my critical judgement	☐	☐	☐
selected relevant key quotations to support my critical judgement	☐	☐	☐
analysed my evidence effectively	☐	☐	☐

Look over all of your work in this unit. Note ✎ down the **three** most important things to remember when writing your response.

1. ....
2. ....
3. ....

Need more practice?

Here is another exam-style question, this time relating to Act 2 Scene 3 of *Romeo and Juliet* on page 75 (Extract C).

Exam-style question

Starting with this extract, explore how Shakespeare presents Friar Lawrence in *Romeo and Juliet*.

Write about:

- how Shakespeare presents Friar Lawrence in this extract
- how Shakespeare presents Friar Lawrence in the play as a whole.

(30 marks)
AO4 (4 marks)

Write ✎ your response to this question.

You'll find some suggested points to refer to in the Answers section.

How confident do you feel about each of these **skills?** Colour ✎ in the bars.

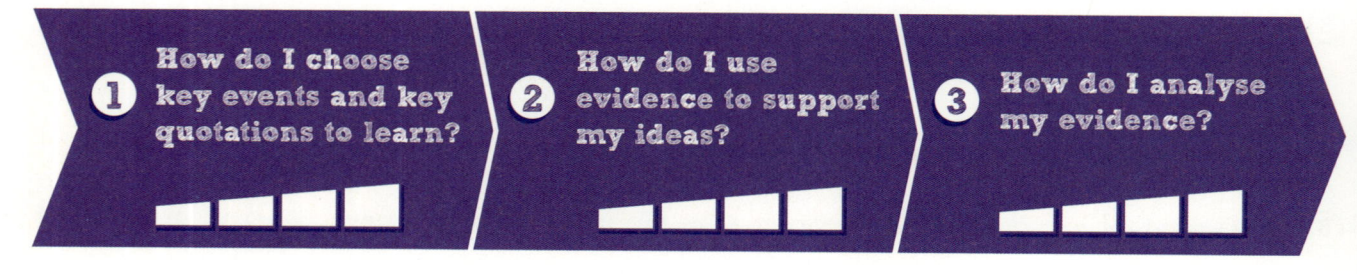

1 How do I choose key events and key quotations to learn?

2 How do I use evidence to support my ideas?

3 How do I analyse my evidence?

48   Unit 6 Writing your response

Get started

Analyse the language, form and structure used by a writer to create meanings and effects (AO2)

7 Commenting on the structure of the play

This unit will help you to comment on Shakespeare's structural choices in *Romeo and Juliet*. The skills you will build are to:

- identify significant structural features of the play
- explore the impact of some of the structural features of the play
- build comments on the play's structure into your analysis.

In the exam you will face a question like the one below. This is about the extract on the next page. At the end of the unit you will **write your own response** to this question.

Exam-style question

Starting with this extract, explore how Shakespeare presents reckless behaviour in *Romeo and Juliet*.

Write about:

- how Shakespeare presents reckless behaviour at this moment in the play
- how Shakespeare presents reckless behaviour in the play as a whole.

(30 marks)
AO4 (4 marks)

Before you tackle the question you will work through three key questions in the **skills boosts** to help you comment on the structure of the play.

1. How can I comment on the structure of the play?
2. How do I comment on the impact of structure?
3. How do I analyse the writer's use of structure?

Read the extract on the next page from Act 3 Scene 1 of *Romeo and Juliet*.

As you read, think about the following:

What has happened before this scene? What happens after this scene?

How does Shakespeare present Mercutio and Tybalt in this extract?

How does Shakespeare present reckless behaviour in this extract?

Unit 7 Commenting on the structure of the play   49

Get started

Exam-style question

Read the following extract from Act 3 Scene 1 of *Romeo and Juliet*.

At this point in the play Romeo and Juliet have fallen in love and married in secret. Benvolio and Mercutio are out on the street in the heat of the day when they meet Tybalt and his companions.

Extract A | Act 3 Scene 1 of *Romeo and Juliet*

Enter TYBALT, with other Capulets and servants.

BENVOLIO
By my head, here come the Capulets!
MERCUTIO
By my heel, I care not.
TYBALT
(To his men) Follow me close, for I will speak to them.
To MERCUTIO and BENVOLIO) Gentlemen, good e'en:
5   a word with one of you.
MERCUTIO
And but one word with one of us? Couple it with
something; make it a word and a blow.
TYBALT
You shall find me apt enough to that, sir, an you will give
me occasion.
MERCUTIO
10 Could you not take some occasion without giving?
TYBALT
Mercutio, thou consortest with Romeo –
MERCUTIO
Consort! What, dost thou make us minstrels? And thou
make minstrels of us, look to hear nothing but discords.
Here's *my* fiddlestick! *(Moving his hand to his sword)* –
15 Here's that shall make you dance. 'Zounds, consort!
BENVOLIO
We talk here in the public haunt of men!
Either withdraw unto some private place,
Or reason coldly of your grievances,
Or else depart. Here all eyes gaze on us.
MERCUTIO
20 Men's eyes were made to look, and let them gaze.
I will not budge for no man's pleasure, I.
Enter ROMEO.
TYBALT
Well, peace be with you, sir. Here comes my man.

Unit 7 Commenting on the structure of the play

Skills boost

1 How can I comment on the structure of the play?

Romeo and Juliet is a tragedy, which means it portrays the tragic downfall of key characters and has an unhappy ending. To comment effectively on the structure of the play, you will need to identify the way in which Shakespeare uses structural features to manipulate the audience's reaction to those tragic events.

1 a Think about how Shakespeare has structured the play to manipulate his audience. Add some or all of the words below, and/or some of your own ideas, to the flow chart beneath.

| romance | killing | revenge | banishment | marriage | conflict | suicide |
| violence | advice | plan | feud | fate | execution | threat |

Beginning
Shakespeare engages the audience's attention with ....

Middle
Shakespeare holds the audience's attention with ....

End
Shakespeare creates a tragic conclusion by ....

b At which point in the play will the audience feel the most tension? Why will they feel tense at this point?

....

2 Fate, or chance, plays an important role in the lives of Romeo and Juliet. The Prologue tells the audience at the start that they are fated to fall in love, but also to die tragically.

> Think about what goes wrong with their plans to be together.

a Look at the 'chance' events in the flow chart below. Add two more.

| Romeo goes to the ball to see Rosaline, but meets Juliet first. | | | Romeo thinks Juliet is dead, and kills himself. |

b How does Shakespeare use the idea of fate to structure the play and manipulate the audience's feelings? Write one or two sentences outlining your ideas.

....

Unit 7 Commenting on the structure of the play

Skills boost

2 How do I comment on the impact of structure?

In your response, you will need to comment on the impact of Shakespeare's structural choices. To do this effectively, make sure you explore a wide range of structural features used in the play.

1 Structural effects can be achieved simply by sequencing key events in a certain order. But Shakespeare uses many other structural features in *Romeo and Juliet* to manipulate audience response.

   a Match the student comments about impact on the right to the structural features on the left.

A The Prologue gives away the plot and the ending.	**a** This links to the idea of fate, as events are rushed and seem out of the characters' control.
B The play starts with servants, rather than with important characters.	**b** This emphasises the tragedy of the serious moments.
C Shakespeare often puts comic scenes before significant events.	**c** This shows that the feud is serious as it affects every level of society.
D The story takes place over only four days.	**d** This creates a sense of anticipation for the audience.

   b For option C above, note down **two** examples of comic scenes or speeches that come before important events.

   [   ]   [   ]

2 The play is structured so that the audience often knows things that some of the characters do not. This is called **dramatic irony**.

   a Identify **two** instances of dramatic irony in *Romeo and Juliet*.

   [   ]

   b For **one** of the examples you identified in part **a** above, write **one** or **two** sentences exploring the impact that the dramatic irony would have on an audience at that point in the play.

   ....

   ....

   ....

52   Unit 7 Commenting on the structure of the play

Skills boost

3. How do I analyse the writer's use of structure?

You can build effective comments on structure into your analysis of the play.

Look at some sentences taken from one student's response to an exam-style question.

Exam-style question

Explore how Shakespeare presents reckless behaviour in *Romeo and Juliet*.

> Mercutio is presented as reckless at the start of Act 3 when Benvolio warns him that the Capulets are likely to be around. Rather than being sensible, he remains in the square, creating humour by making up ridiculous reasons why Benvolio has picked quarrels with people.

1 Now look at some sentences focusing on the play's structure that could be added to this paragraph.

A Mercutio then becomes angry when Tybalt arrives, challenging him to fight, and this changes the mood of the scene from comic to dramatic.

B This comic moment causes tension as the audience can sense that Mercutio's reckless mood may result in a dramatic confrontation when Tybalt appears.

C This creates tension for the audience, who already know from the Prologue that the play will end in tragedy, so they anticipate a serious, perhaps deadly, conflict.

D This is perhaps the key moment in the play as Mercutio's reckless challenge to Tybalt sets in motion the chain of events that leads to the eventual tragedy.

a Which **two** sentences would you add to the paragraph above to explore the impact of structure? Tick ✓ them.

b Mark ✏ where you would add them by writing the letter **A**, **B**, **C**, etc. on the student's response paragraph above.

2 Now look at another paragraph taken from the same student's response.

> Another instance of reckless behaviour is when Juliet defies her father and refuses to marry Paris. Juliet's father wants her to marry without delay, but she asks him to show 'patience' and begs him to listen. Juliet started the play as an innocent, child-like character but the way she stands up to her parents shows that she is rapidly developing into an independent young woman.

a Write ✏ **one** or **two** sentences that could be added to this paragraph, to develop the analysis by focusing on the play's structure.

> Think about the short timeframe of the play, as well as about dramatic irony.

....
....
....

b Add ✏ an asterisk * to the student's response paragraph above to show where you would insert your sentence(s).

Unit 7 Commenting on the structure of the play

Get back on track

Commenting on the structure of the play

To comment on the structure of the play, you need to:
- identify significant structural choices that Shakespeare has made
- consider how Shakespeare has used these structural choices to manipulate the audience's response to the characters and events in the play
- link these structural features and their impact to the focus of the question.

Look at this exam-style question you saw at the start of the unit.

> **Exam-style question**
>
> Starting with this extract, explore how Shakespeare presents reckless behaviour in *Romeo and Juliet*.
>
> Write about:
> - how Shakespeare presents reckless behaviour at this moment in the play
> - how Shakespeare presents reckless behaviour in the play as a whole.

Now look at a paragraph taken from one student's response to the question.

> The most obvious type of reckless behaviour in 'Romeo and Juliet' is that which leads to violent conflict. The play starts with the Capulet servant, Sampson, boasting of what he will do to the Montagues. By opening the play in this way, with the servants rather than with important characters, Shakespeare is showing how significant the feud is as it obviously affects all levels of society. Despite the other servant, Gregory, telling him that the quarrel is not with them but with their 'masters', Sampson continues and eventually provokes a public brawl, which involves important characters like Benvolio, Tybalt and Lord Capulet. By starting the play in this way, Shakespeare suggests that all parts of Verona society are capable of reckless behaviour. This violence would make the audience tense, as the scene comes immediately after the Prologue warns that 'new mutiny' will end in tragedy.

1. What significant structural choices does the student explore in this paragraph? Underline them and label them '**structure**'.

2. Identify the part of the paragraph in which the student has responded to the focus of the question. Underline it and label it '**question**'.

3. Identify the part of the paragraph in which the student has used specific events as evidence. Underline it and label it '**evidence**'.

Get back on track

Your turn!

You are now going to **write your own answer** in response to the exam-style question.

> **Exam-style question**
>
> Starting with this extract, explore how Shakespeare presents reckless behaviour in *Romeo and Juliet*.
>
> Write about:
> - how Shakespeare presents reckless behaviour at this moment in the play
> - how Shakespeare presents reckless behaviour in the play as a whole.
>
> (30 marks)
> AO4 (4 marks)

1. Write **one** or **two** sentences summarising your critical judgement in response to the question.

   ....

   ....

2. Which key events and/or quotations from the extract on page 50 would support your critical judgement?

3. Which key events and evidence from the play as a whole would support your critical judgement?

4. Look at all the evidence you have gathered. Think about how you could use it to comment on:
   - **language and structure** in your quotations
   - **character**
   - the **theme** you are exploring: reckless behaviour
   - the **structure** of the play
   - Shakespeare's **intention**: how might the audience respond?

   Annotate your evidence with your ideas.

5. Now write your response to the exam-style question above on paper.

Unit 7 Commenting on the structure of the play

Review your skills

Get back on track

Check up

Review your response to the exam-style question on page 55. Tick ✓ the column to show how well you think you have done each of the following.

	Not quite ✓	Nearly there ✓	Got it! ✓
selected relevant evidence, commenting on character and theme	☐	☐	☐
identified relevant and significant structural features of the play	☐	☐	☐
commented on the impact of those structural features	☐	☐	☐
linked my comments on structure to the focus of the question	☐	☐	☐

Look over all of your work in this unit. Note ✎ down the **three** most important things to remember when commenting on the structure of the play.

1. ....
2. ....
3. ....

Need more practice?

Look at this exam-style question, this time relating to Act 1 Scene 5 of *Romeo and Juliet* on page 76 (Extract D).

Exam-style question

Starting with this extract, explore how Shakespeare presents hatred in *Romeo and Juliet*.
Write about:
- how Shakespeare presents hatred at this moment in the play
- how Shakespeare presents hatred in the play as a whole.

(30 marks)
AO4 (4 marks)

Plan ✎ your response to the question.
- Which key events will you focus on? Note them down.
- Which key structural features of the play will you focus on? Add them to your plan.
- What impact do these structural features have on the presentation of hatred in *Romeo and Juliet*? Note your ideas.

You'll find some suggested ideas in the Answers section.

How confident do you feel about each of these **skills**? Colour ✎ in the bars.

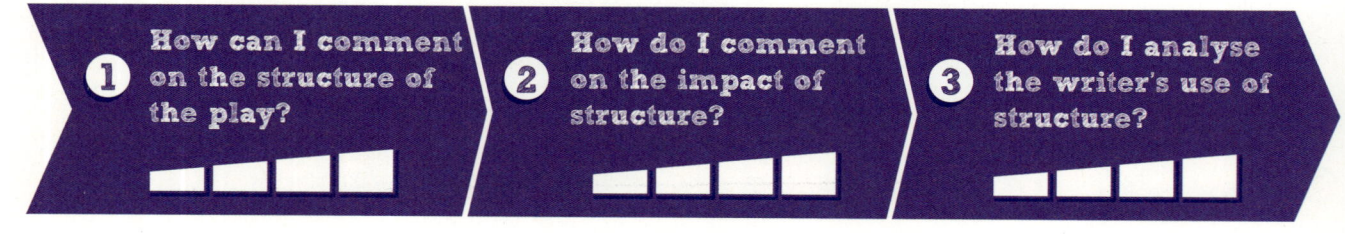

1. How can I comment on the structure of the play?
2. How do I comment on the impact of structure?
3. How do I analyse the writer's use of structure?

56   Unit 7 Commenting on the structure of the play

Get started

Show understanding of the relationships between texts and the contexts in which they were written (AO3)

8 Commenting on context

This unit will help you to show your understanding of the play's context: its relationship with the time the play was written and first performed. The skills you will build are to:

- understand the relationship between the play and its context
- explain the impact of context on different elements of the play
- incorporate comments on context into your writing about the play.

In the exam you will face a question like the one below. This is about the extract on the next page. At the end of the unit you will **write your own response** to this question.

> **Exam-style question**
>
> Starting with this extract, explore how far you think Shakespeare presents Lord Capulet as a caring father.
>
> Write about:
> - how Shakespeare presents Lord Capulet in this extract
> - how Shakespeare presents Lord Capulet in the play as a whole.
>
> (30 marks)
> AO4 (4 marks)

Before you tackle the question you will work through three key questions in the **skills boosts** to help you write about the play's context.

1. How do I know which contextual ideas to write about?
2. How do I comment on context?
3. How do I build my comments on context into my analysis?

Read the extract on the next page from Act 3 Scene 4 of *Romeo and Juliet*.

As you read, think about the following:

- What has happened before this scene? What happens after this scene?
- How does Shakespeare present Lord Capulet in this extract?
- How does Shakespeare present marriage in this scene?

Unit 8 Commenting on context   57

Get started

> **Exam-style question**
>
> Read the following extract from Act 3 Scene 4 of *Romeo and Juliet*.
>
> At this point in the play Lord Capulet has decided to agree to Paris's request to marry Juliet.

Extract A | Act 3 Scene 4 of *Romeo and Juliet*

Enter CAPULET, LADY CAPULET and PARIS.

CAPULET
Things have fall'n out, sir, so unluckily,
That we have had no time to move our daughter.
Look you, she loved her kinsman Tybalt dearly,
And so did I. Well, we were born to die.
5   'Tis very late. She'll not come down tonight.
I promise you, but for your company,
I would have been abed an hour ago.

PARIS
These times of woe afford no time to woo.
Madam good night. Commend me to your daughter.

LADY CAPULET
10   I will, and know her mind early tomorrow.
Tonight she's mewed up to her heaviness.

PARIS goes, but CAPULET calls him back.

CAPULET
Sir Paris! – I will make a desperate tender
Of my child's love: I think she will be ruled
In all respects by me – nay more, I doubt it not.
15   Wife, go you to her ere you go to bed.
Acquaint her here of my son Paris' love,
And bid her – mark you me? – on Wednesday next--
But soft, what day is this?

PARIS
           Monday my lord.

CAPULET
20   Monday, ah ha! Well, Wednesday is too soon.
O' Thursday let it be. O' Thursday, tell her,
She shall be married to this noble earl.
Will you be ready? Do you like this haste?
We'll keep no great ado – a friend or two.
25   For hark you, Tybalt being slain so late,
It may be thought we held him carelessly,
Being our kinsman, if we revel much.
Therefore we'll have some half a dozen friends,
And there an end.

Skills boost

1 How do I know which contextual ideas to write about?

You need to be aware of all the different contexts of *Romeo and Juliet* on which you could comment so that you can choose those that are most relevant to the focus of the question.

(1) Look at some of the features of *Romeo and Juliet* and the time in which it was written. Tick ✓ any that are relevant to the play, and cross ✗ any that are not.

Shakespeare and Elizabethan society

A Shakespeare did not invent the story of Romeo and Juliet; many details came from a well-known poem. ☐

B Romeo and Juliet was written around 1595 and was one of Shakespeare's most popular plays. ☐

C While the play was being written, society was rather unstable and there were public riots in protest at taxes and lack of food. ☐

Elizabethan theatres

D An Elizabethan audience often chatted, ate and wandered about during plays so they needed plenty of action and drama to keep them interested. ☐

E For Shakespeare's audience, Italy was an exotic, distant country associated with wealth and romance. ☐

F Many strolling troupes went about the country and commonly consisted of three or four men, and a boy who took the women's parts. ☐

G The Elizabethan general public would pay 1 penny to stand in theatres and the wealthy would pay more to sit in the galleries, often using cushions for comfort. ☐

16th–17th-century attitudes

H It was a patriarchal society: that is, one ruled by men, who held total power over their wives and children. ☐

I Young women were expected to marry as a way to improve their family's status and were usually married between the ages of 16 and 18. ☐

J Wealthy children were often raised by a 'wet nurse' and had little daily contact with their parents. ☐

K Family honour was important to wealthy families; men would have been expected to uphold their family's honour. ☐

(2) Now think about some of these key events and characters in the play.

| Romeo | Juliet | The death of Mercutio | Paris asking to marry Juliet | The opening fight scene |

Annotate ✏️ the diagram with these words, using arrows to link them to all the relevant elements of context.

Unit 8 Commenting on context

Skills boost

2 How do I comment on context?

An effective comment on context can focus on how it relates to the events of the play and its impact on different audiences.

Look at the beginning of one student's paragraph exploring how Lord Capulet is presented in Act 1 Scene 2.

> Lord Capulet calls Juliet 'the hopeful lady of my earth' and says that he will only consent to a marriage with Paris if his daughter actually falls in love with him.

1 Now look at some different students' comments on the context of the play in this scene.

> **A** This suggests that, although Lord Capulet is a typical patriarchal father of the time, he does actually care about Juliet's happiness.

> **B** Here, Shakespeare suggests that Capulet is a caring parent as most marriages in the sixteenth century were based only on increasing a family's wealth and status, not on romantic love.

> **C** To a seventeenth-century audience, Lord Capulet's insistence that Juliet be in love before she marry would have seemed unusual, whereas a twenty-first-century audience would see his attitude as that of a caring father.

a Which comment does what? Circle (A) or cross out (~~A~~) the letters in the table below.

Context	Comment		
identifies the time in which the play was written	A	B	C
identifies a relevant belief, attitude or situation at that time	A	B	C
considers Shakespeare's intention	A	B	C
considers the impact on an audience	A	B	C
compares today's audience with Shakespeare's audience	A	B	C

b Which of the comments above would you use when writing about Lord Capulet in Act 1 Scene 2? Tick ✓ **one or more**.

2 Look at these sentences from the beginning of another student's paragraph about Lady Capulet in Act 1 Scene 3.

> When the audience is introduced to Lady Capulet, she is presented as a distant parent because she appears to know less about her daughter than Juliet's nurse does.

a Write ✏ **one** or **two** sentences adding a contextual comment to the paragraph.

....

....

b Check your comment. Does it achieve all or most of the criteria listed in question **1** **a**? Adjust ✏ it as necessary.

Unit 8 Commenting on context

Skills boost

3 How do I build my comments on context into my analysis?

You do not need to make contextual comments in every paragraph of your response, but you do need to make them relevant to your analysis of the play.

Look at the opening of a paragraph from a student's response, commenting on the presentation of family relationships in Act 3 Scene 5.

> In Act 3 Scene 5, Juliet begs her mother not to send her away, calling her 'sweet my mother'. However, Lady Capulet refuses to listen, saying 'I have done with thee'.

(1) Now look at some sentences you could add to this paragraph.

A This exchange shows how disgusted Lady Capulet is by her daughter's disobedience.

a A modern audience would be extremely shocked at this point, as we now have an expectation that mothers stick by their children no matter what they do or say.

B This cold response shows how distant Lady Capulet is as a mother.

b Shakespeare's audience would have understood this as women were completely dependent on men at that time.

C Juliet's desperate appeal to her mother shows how frightened she is to be cast out by her family.

c This would not have surprised a sixteenth-century audience, as women were expected to be completely subservient and respectful to their husbands.

D Lady Capulet's response shows how far she will go to back up her husband.

d Any challenge to parental authority would have shocked a sixteenth-century audience, who expected children to obey their parents in every respect.

a The sentences either comment on the **impact** of the evidence in the paragraph or comment on the play's **context**. Decide which heading ('Impact' or 'Context') to add ✏️ above each of the columns of text.

b Which comments on context are relevant to which comments on impact? Draw ✏️ lines linking them.

c Which of the sentences above would you include in a paragraph analysing how Shakespeare presents Lady Capulet and Juliet in Act 3 Scene 5 and in what order would you sequence them? Write ✏️ the sentence order here.

☐ ☐ ☐ ☐ ☐ ☐ ☐

Unit 8 Commenting on context   **61**

Get back on track

Commenting on context

To comment effectively on context, you need to:
- use a relevant contextual point to develop your analysis of a key point, supported by evidence
- explore what this contextual idea adds to your understanding of Shakespeare's intention and his audience's response.

Look at this exam-style question you saw at the start of the unit.

Exam-style question

Starting with this extract, explore how far you think Shakespeare presents Lord Capulet as a caring father.

Write about:
- how Shakespeare presents Lord Capulet in this extract
- how Shakespeare presents Lord Capulet in the play as a whole.

① Now look at a paragraph focusing on the play as a whole, taken from one student's response to the question.

> When Lord Capulet hears Juliet's refusal to marry Paris, he becomes very angry, first asking why 'Doth she not give us thanks?', then insulting her: 'you green-sickness carrion', and then threatening her: 'My fingers itch'. This is a very disturbing moment in the play for a modern audience as it suggests he feels physical force against his daughter is acceptable. However, because Shakespeare's audience lived in a patriarchal society, where men were in total control of their families, they would be more shocked by Juliet's disobedience. Shakespeare wants his audience to be shocked at this point, as it makes Juliet's future all the more uncertain and therefore more dramatic.

- uses a key event as evidence
- uses a quotation as evidence
- comments on the impact of the evidence
- identifies a relevant contextual point
- explores Shakespeare's intention in the light of this contextual point
- explores the audience's response in the light of this contextual point

Can you identify all the different things the student has included in this paragraph? Link 🖉 the annotations to the paragraph to show where the student has included them.

62   Unit 8 Commenting on context

Get back on track

Your turn!

You are now going to **write your own answer** in response to the exam-style question.

> **Exam-style question**
>
> Starting with this extract, explore how far you think Shakespeare presents Lord Capulet as a caring father.
>
> Write about:
> - how Shakespeare presents Lord Capulet in this extract
> - how Shakespeare presents Lord Capulet in the play as a whole.
>
> (30 marks)
> AO4 (4 marks)

1. Write ✏️ **one** or **two** sentences, summarising your critical judgement in response to the question: Does Shakespeare present Lord Capulet as a caring father?

   ....

   ....

2. Which key events in the play would support your critical judgement? Note ✏️ them below.

   [   ]

3. Look at all the evidence you have gathered. Think about:
   - what your evidence suggests about Lord Capulet
   - what your evidence suggests about Shakespeare's intention: how might the audience respond at this point?

   Annotate ✏️ your evidence with your ideas.

4. Now think about the relevant contextual points you could make in your response. Annotate ✏️ your evidence with your ideas.

5. Look at your annotated evidence.

   a. Which are your strongest ideas? Tick ✓ them.

   b. Number ✏️ the ideas that you have ticked, and sequence them here to build an argument that supports your critical judgement. ☐ ☐ ☐ ☐ ☐

6. Now write ✏️ your response to the exam-style question above on paper.

Unit 8 Commenting on context

Review your skills

Check up

Review your response to the exam-style question on page 63. Tick ✓ the column to show how well you think you have done each of the following.

	Not quite	Nearly there	Got it!
identified relevant contextual points	☐	☐	☐
used relevant contextual points to develop my analysis	☐	☐	☐
explored Shakespeare's intention and the audience's response in the light of the play's context	☐	☐	☐

Look over all of your work in this unit. Note down the **three** most important things to remember when commenting on context.

1. ....
2. ....
3. ....

Need more practice?

Look at this exam-style question, this time relating to Act 1 Scene 3 on page 77 (Extract E).

Exam-style question

Starting with this extract, explore how Shakespeare presents marriage in *Romeo and Juliet*.

Write about:
- how Shakespeare presents marriage in this extract
- how Shakespeare presents marriage in the play as a whole.

(30 marks)
AO4 (4 marks)

Write your response to this question.
You'll find some suggested points to refer to in the Answers section.

How confident do you feel about each of these **skills?** Colour in the bars.

1. How do I know which contextual ideas to write about?
2. How do I comment on context?
3. How do I build my comments on context into my analysis?

Get started

Use a range of vocabulary and sentence structures for clarity, purpose and effect (AO4)

9 Developing a critical writing style

This unit will help you to express your ideas about *Romeo and Juliet* as clearly and precisely as possible. The skills you will build are to:

- select vocabulary to express your ideas precisely
- link your ideas to express them clearly
- extend your sentences to develop ideas more fully.

In the exam you will face questions like the one below. This is about the extract on the next page. At the end of the unit you will **write one paragraph** in response to this question.

> **Exam-style question**
>
> Starting with this extract, how does Shakespeare present Juliet in the play *Romeo and Juliet*?
>
> Write about:
> - how Shakespeare presents Juliet in this speech
> - how Shakespeare presents Juliet in the play as a whole.
>
> (30 marks)
> AO4 (4 marks)

Before you tackle the question you will work through three key questions in the **skills boosts** to help you develop a critical writing style.

1. How do I choose vocabulary which expresses my ideas precisely?
2. How can I link my ideas to express them more clearly?
3. How can I extend my sentences to develop my ideas more fully?

Read the extract on the next page from Act 4 Scene 3 of *Romeo and Juliet*.

As you read, think about the following:

- What has happened before this scene? What happens after this scene?
- How does Shakespeare present Juliet's thoughts and feelings in this scene?
- How does Shakespeare present ideas about death and dying in this scene?

Unit 9 Developing a critical writing style 65

Get started

> **Exam-style question**
>
> Read the following extract from Act 4 Scene 3 of *Romeo and Juliet* and then answer the question on page 65.
>
> At this point in the play Juliet is about to take the potion given to her by Friar Lawrence in order to pretend that she is dead.

Extract A | Act 4 Scene 3 of *Romeo and Juliet*

JULIET
Farewell. – God knows when we shall meet again.
I have a faint cold fear thrills through my veins,
That almost freezes up the heat of life.
I'll call them back again to comfort me.
5 *(She calls)* Nurse! – What should she do here?
My dismal scene I needs must act alone.
Come, vial.
What if this mixture do not work at all?
Shall I be married then tomorrow morning?
10 No, no. – *(Taking out her knife)* This shall forbid it.
(Placing the knife inside the curtain by her bed)
Lie thou there.
What if it be a poison which the friar
Subtly hath ministered to have me dead,
Lest in this marriage he should be dishonoured
15 Because he married me before to Romeo?
I fear it is. And yet methinks it should not,
For he hath still been tried a holy man.
How if when I am laid into the tomb,
I wake before the time that Romeo
20 Come to redeem me? There's a fearful point!
Shall I not then be stifled in the vault,
To whose foul mouth no healthsome air breathes in,
And there die strangled ere my Romeo comes?
Or, if I live, is it not very like
25 The horrible conceit of death and night,
Together with the terror of the place –
As in a vault, an ancient receptacle,
Where, for this many hundred years, the bones
Of all my buried ancestors are packed –
30 Where bloody Tybalt, yet but green in earth,
Lies festering in his shroud – where, as they say,
At some hours in the night spirits resort –

Skills boost

1. How do I choose vocabulary that expresses my ideas precisely?

You need to choose precise vocabulary to describe your response to the play accurately.

1 Look at this list of key scenes in the play.

Scene		Character	Audience
1.1	Romeo tells Benvolio he is suffering from unrequited love.		
1.3	The Nurse recalls events of Juliet's life.		
2.2	The balcony scene.		
3.1	Romeo decides to fight Tybalt.		
5.3	Romeo and Juliet are found dead.		

a Choose a word from the word box to describe how relationships and/or love are presented in the scene. Write ✏ it under the scene.

romantic	cruel	nurturing	honourable	eternal
idealistic	distant	tender	loyal	doomed
exciting	domineering	benevolent	principled	guilty
unrealistic	conflicted	affectionate	pure	bleak
fairy tale	dictatorial	compassionate	sentimental	tragic

b Now think about the characters in these scenes and choose at least one word to describe how they are presented. Add ✏ to the Character column.

arrogant	harsh	innocent	vulnerable
brutal	amused	indulgent	forbearing
hostile	protective	verbose	despairing
passionate	embarrassed	impulsive	impetuous

c Now think about what Shakespeare wanted the audience to feel about these characters. Choose one or two words from the box to describe their reaction and write ✏ it in the Audience column.

excitement	affection	horror	amusement	admiration
anticipation	relief	disgust	shock	sorrow
joy	empathy	anger	sentiment	sympathy

Unit 9 Developing a critical writing style

Skills boost

2. How can I link my ideas to express them more clearly?

You can use conjunctions to link your ideas, helping you to express your ideas more clearly and fluently.

Coordinating conjunctions link related or contrasting ideas:

and | but | or | so

Subordinating conjunctions express more complex connections:
- an explanation, e.g. because | in order to
- a comparison, e.g. although | whereas
- a sequence, e.g. when | after | until

1 Look at these pairs of sentences.

A
- Romeo meets Juliet at the ball. They fall in love immediately.
- Benvolio is hesitant about remaining in the street. Mercutio has no such doubts. Mercutio provokes a fight with Tybalt.
- Lord Capulet loses his temper with Juliet. She refuses to marry Paris. Lord Capulet threatens to disown Juliet.

B
- When Romeo meets Juliet at the ball, they fall in love immediately.
- Benvolio is hesitant about remaining in the street, whereas Mercutio has no such doubts and provokes a fight with Tybalt.
- Lord Capulet loses his temper with Juliet because she refuses to marry Paris, so he threatens to disown her.

a Circle (A) the **conjunctions** in the sentences labelled B.

b Tick (✓) the version of each sentence that you feel is more clearly and fluently expressed.

2 Rewrite ✎ these pairs of sentences, using a conjunction to link them. Remember to choose and position your conjunction carefully to express each idea as clearly and fluently as possible.

| The Nurse seems excited to see Romeo and Juliet falling in love, and acts as their go-between. | **+** | She does warn Romeo not to hurt Juliet. |

| Juliet refuses to marry her father's choice of husband. | **+** | Paris is presented as a suitable husband. |

| Lady Capulet is dismissive of Juliet's grief for Tybalt. | **+** | Lord Capulet is caring and compares her to a small boat in a storm. |

Unit 9 Developing a critical writing style

Skills boost

3. How can I extend my sentences to develop my ideas more fully?

One way to extend your sentences, and develop your ideas, is by using conjunctions. Other ways include:
- using present participles: a verb ending in *–ing*
- using the pronoun *which*.

Conjunctions	and	but	when	as	before	after
	although	if	whereas	unless	because	since

You could complete this sentence:

> Friar Lawrence offers support to both Romeo and Juliet…

- using this conjunction: **but** does express doubts about their desire to wed so quickly.
- or a present participle: **suggesting** a plan to help them be together.
- or *which*: **which** he believes is the best way to end the public feuding.

1 Complete ✏️ this sentence in three different ways.

> Mercutio is killed by Tybalt with a hidden thrust under Romeo's arm…

a Use a conjunction: ....

b Use a present participle: ....

c Use *which*: ....

You can use *which* or a present participle to avoid repeatedly beginning sentences with 'This suggests…' or 'This shows…'.

For example:

| The Nurse shows a great affection for Juliet. **This suggests** she has a more serious side. | The Nurse shows a great affection for Juliet, **which suggests** she has a more serious side. | The Nurse shows a great affection for Juliet, **suggesting** she has a more serious side. |

2 Change ✏️ these sentences to make them a single sentence, using a present participle or *which*.

> Mercutio often repeats Romeo's words and makes bawdy jokes. This encourages the audience to see him as light-hearted.

> The letter from Friar Lawrence fails to reach Romeo in Mantua. This creates the impression that fate is again controlling the young lovers' lives.

Unit 9 Developing a critical writing style

Developing a critical writing style

> To express your ideas clearly and precisely, you can:
> - select vocabulary that expresses your ideas precisely
> - link your ideas using conjunctions, present participles, etc. to develop and express them clearly.

Now look at this exam-style question you saw on page 65.

Exam-style question

Starting with this extract, how does Shakespeare present Juliet in the play *Romeo and Juliet*?

Write about:
- how Shakespeare presents Juliet in this speech
- how Shakespeare presents Juliet in the play as a whole.

1 Look at a short paragraph from one student's response to the question.

> *Once she has married Romeo, Juliet is presented as good. She refuses to marry Paris. Juliet stands up to her father. He gets angry. He calls her a 'baggage'. This presents him as a bad father. The audience would like this, as they would like Juliet. Juliet's Nurse then tells her to marry Paris. Juliet sends her away. This suggests she is now lonely but brave.*

a Underline (A) **at least three** examples of vocabulary which could be more precise.

b Note down in the margin **at least three** alternative vocabulary choices for each one.

c Highlight any of the sentences which you feel should be linked or developed to improve the clarity and precision of the writing.

d Write an improved version of this paragraph, either by adjusting the text above or by rewriting it in the space below.

Get back on track

Your turn!

You are now going to **write one paragraph** in response to the exam-style question.

Exam-style question

Starting with this extract, how does Shakespeare present Juliet in the play *Romeo and Juliet*?

Write about:
- how Shakespeare presents Juliet in this speech
- how Shakespeare presents Juliet in the play as a whole.

(30 marks)

AO4 (4 marks)

1. **a** Think about some of the things that Juliet does, then decide how she is presented. ✓

Juliet...	Not courageous?	In the middle?	Courageous?
says she is not interested in marriage	☐	☐	☐
meets Romeo at the ball	☐	☐	☐
suggests to Romeo that they marry	☐	☐	☐
refuses to marry Paris	☐	☐	☐
sends her nurse away	☐	☐	☐
begs Friar Lawrence to help her	☐	☐	☐
decides to take the potion	☐	☐	☐
kills herself	☐	☐	☐

b For each of the above events from the play, choose **one** or **two** ambitious words to describe how Juliet is presented at that point. Note ✎ them on paper.

c Now choose **one** or **two** key events that you can explore in your response to the exam-style question. You could choose from the list above, or use your own ideas. Add ✎ them to your notes.

d Look at each of your chosen events. What themes are relevant? Add ✎ your ideas to your notes, using ambitious vocabulary.

e Use your ideas to write ✎ **one** paragraph in response to the exam-style question on paper.

2. When you have finished writing, read over your paragraph and underline Ⓐ:

   a where you have used ambitious vocabulary

   b where you have joined sentences effectively

   c where you have developed your sentences to make your writing more fluent.

Unit 9 Developing a critical writing style

Get back on track

Review your skills

Check up

Review your response to the exam-style question on page 71. Tick ✓ the column to show how well you think you have done each of the following.

	Not quite ✓	Nearly there ✓	Got it! ✓
selected precise vocabulary	☐	☐	☐
linked and developed my ideas clearly and precisely using conjunctions, present participles, etc.	☐	☐	☐

Look over all of your work in this unit. Note ✏️ down the **three** most important things to remember when trying to express your ideas as clearly and precisely as possible.

1. ....
2. ....
3. ....

Need more practice?

You can EITHER:

1. Look again at your paragraph written in response to the exam-style question on page 71. Rewrite ✏️ it, experimenting with different vocabulary choices and sentence structures, linking your ideas in different ways. Which are most effective in expressing your ideas clearly and precisely?

AND/OR:

2. Choose a **second** point from the suggestions on page 71. Write ✏️ a further paragraph in response to the exam-style question, focusing closely on your vocabulary choice and sentence structures.

How confident do you feel about each of these **skills?** Colour ✏️ in the bars.

1. How do I choose vocabulary that expresses my ideas precisely?
2. How can I link my ideas to express them more clearly?
3. How can I extend my sentences to develop my ideas more fully?

Unit 9 Developing a critical writing style

More practice questions

Units 1 and 2

Exam-style question

Read the following extract from Act 5 Scene 3 of *Romeo and Juliet* and then answer the question that follows.

At this point in the play Romeo is at Juliet's tomb and has just realised that he has killed Paris.

Extract A | Act 5 Scene 3 of *Romeo and Juliet*

ROMEO
In faith, I will. Let me peruse this face.
Mercutio's kinsman, noble County Paris!
What said my man, when my betossèd soul
Did not attend him as we rode? I think
5   He told me Paris should have married Juliet.
Said he not so? Or did I dream it so?
Or am I mad, hearing him talk of Juliet,
To think it was so? O, give me thy hand,
One writ with me in sour misfortune's book.
10 I'll bury thee in a triumphant grave. –
– A grave? – O, no – a lantern, slaughtered youth! –
For here lies Juliet, and her beauty makes
This vault a feasting presence full of light.
Death, lie thou there, by a dead man interred.
15 *(He lays PARIS's body down, and turns towards JULIET.)*
How oft when men are at the point of death
Have they been merry, which their keepers call
A lightning before death! O, how may I
20 Call this a lightning? O my love, my wife!
Death that hath sucked the honey of thy breath,
Hath had no power yet upon thy beauty.
Thou art not conquered. Beauty's ensign yet
Is crimson in thy lips and in thy cheeks,
25 And death's pale flag is not advanced there.

Starting with this extract, explain how Shakespeare presents feelings of anguish in *Romeo and Juliet*.

Write about:

- how Shakespeare presents feelings of anguish in this speech
- how Shakespeare presents feelings of anguish in the play as a whole.

(30 marks)

AO4 (4 marks)

Unit 1 Which key events in the play would you choose to write about in your response to this question?

Unit 2 Write one or two paragraphs in response to this question, focusing on the extract only.

Units 3 and 4

> **Exam-style question**
>
> Read the following extract from Act 3 Scene 5 of *Romeo and Juliet* and then answer the question that follows.
>
> At this point in the play Juliet has angered her parents by refusing to marry Paris and asks the Nurse for her advice.
>
> **Extract B** | Act 3 Scene 5 of *Romeo and Juliet*
>
> **JULIET**
> O God! – O Nurse, how shall this be prevented?
> My husband is on earth, my faith in heaven.
> How shall that faith return again to earth,
> Unless that husband send it me from heaven
> 5 By leaving earth? Comfort me, counsel me.
> Alack, alack, that heaven should practise stratagems
> Upon so soft a subject as myself!
> What say'st thou? Hast thou not a word of joy?
> Some comfort, nurse?
>
> **NURSE**
> 10   Faith, here it is.
> Romeo is banishèd – and all the world to nothing
> That he dares ne'er come back to challenge you.
> Or if he do, it needs must be by stealth.
> Then, since the case so stands as now it doth,
> 15 I think it best you married with the County.
> O, he's a lovely gentleman!
> Romeo's a dishclout to him. An eagle, madam,
> Hath not so green, so quick, so fair an eye
> As Paris hath. Beshrew my very heart,
> 20 I think you are happy in this second match,
> For it excels your first – or if it did not,
> Your first is dead, or 'twere as good he were,
> As living here, and you no use of him.
>
> **JULIET**
> Speak'st thou from thy heart?
>
> **NURSE**
> 25 And from my soul too – else beshrew them both.
>
> Starting with this extract, explore how Shakespeare presents the Nurse in *Romeo and Juliet*.
>
> Write about:
> - how Shakespeare presents the Nurse in this extract
> - how Shakespeare presents the Nurse in the play as a whole.
>
> (30 marks)
> AO4 (4 marks)

Unit 3 Write **one** or **two** paragraphs in response to this question, focusing on the language and structure **in the extract only.**

Unit 4 Write **one** or **two** paragraphs in response to this question, focusing on the second bullet point: **the play as a whole.**

More practice questions

Units 5 and 6

Exam-style question

Read the following extract from Act 2 Scene 3 of *Romeo and Juliet* and then answer the question that follows.

At this point in the play Romeo has fallen in love with Juliet at the Capulets' ball and is visiting Friar Lawrence.

Extract C | Act 2 Scene 3 of *Romeo and Juliet*

FRIAR LAWRENCE
Be plain, good son, and homely in thy drift;
Riddling confession finds but riddling shrift.

ROMEO
Then plainly know, my heart's dear love is set
On the fair daughter of rich Capulet.
5   As mine on hers, so hers is set on mine,
And all combined – save what thou must combine
By holy marriage. When and where and how
We met, we wooed, and made exchange of vow,
I'll tell thee as we pass. But this I pray,
10 That thou consent to marry us today.

FRIAR LAWRENCE
Holy Saint Francis, what a change is here!
Is Rosaline that thou didst love so dear,
So soon forsaken? Young men's love then lies
Not truly in their hearts, but in their eyes.
15 Jesu Maria, what a deal of brine
Hath washed thy sallow cheeks for Rosaline!
How much salt water thrown away in waste
To season love, that of it doth not taste!
The sun not yet thy sighs from heaven clears,
20 Thy old groans ring yet in my ancient ears –
Lo, here upon thy cheek the stain doth sit
Of an old tear that is not washed off yet.
If e'er thou wast thyself, and these woes thine,
Thou and these woes were all for Rosaline.
25 And art thou changed? Pronounce this sentence then:
Women may fall, when there's no strength in men.

ROMEO
Thou chid'st me oft for loving Rosaline.

FRIAR LAWRENCE
For doting, not for loving, pupil mine.

Starting with this extract, explore how Shakespeare presents Friar Lawrence in *Romeo and Juliet*.

Write about:
- how Shakespeare presents Friar Lawrence in this extract
- how Shakespeare presents Friar Lawrence in the play as a whole.

(30 marks)
AO4 (4 marks)

Unit 5 Plan your response to this question.

Unit 6 Write your response to this question.

Unit 7

> **Exam-style question**

Read the following extract from Act 1 Scene 5 of *Romeo and Juliet* and then answer the question that follows.

At this point in the play Tybalt has recognised Romeo at the Capulets' ball and becomes very angry.

Extract D | Act 1 Scene 5 of *Romeo and Juliet*

TYBALT
This, by his voice, should be a Montague.
Fetch me my rapier, boy.
Exit Page.
        What! – Dares the slave
Come hither, covered with an antic face,
5 To fleer and scorn at our solemnity?
Now, by the stock and honour of my kin,
To strike him dead I hold it not a sin.
CAPULET
Why, how now, kinsman! Wherefore storm you so?
TYBALT
Uncle, this is a Montague, our foe!
10 A villain that is hither come in spite,
To scorn at our solemnity this night.
CAPULET
Young Romeo is it?
TYBALT
        'Tis he, that villain Romeo.
CAPULET
Content thee, gentle coz, let him alone.
15 'A bears him like a portly gentleman –
And, to say truth, Verona brags of him
To be a virtuous and well-governed youth.
I would not, for the wealth of all this town,
Here in my house do him disparagement.
20 Therefore be patient, take no note of him.
It is my will, the which if thou respect,
Show a fair presence and put off these frowns,
And ill-beseeming semblance for a feast.
TYBALT
It fits, when such a villain is a guest.
25 I'll not endure him!
…
Patience perforce with wilful choler meeting
Makes my flesh tremble in their different greeting.
I will withdraw. But this intrusion shall,
Now seeming sweet, convert to bitterest gall!

Starting with this extract, explore how Shakespeare presents hatred in *Romeo and Juliet*.

Write about:

- how Shakespeare presents hatred in this extract
- how Shakespeare presents hatred in the play as a whole.

(30 marks)
AO4 (4 marks)

Unit 7 Plan your response to the question.

More practice questions

Unit 8

> **Exam-style question**

Read the following extract from Act 1 Scene 3 of *Romeo and Juliet* and then answer the question that follows.

At this point in the play Lady Capulet is telling Juliet that Paris has asked for her hand in marriage.

Extract E | Act 1 Scene 3 of *Romeo and Juliet*

LADY CAPULET
What say you? Can you love the gentleman?
This night you shall behold him at our feast.
Read o'er the volume of young Paris' face,
And find delight writ there with beauty's pen.
5   Examine every married lineament,
And see how one another lends content –
And what obscured in this fair volume lies,
Find written in the margent of his eyes.
This precious book of love, this unbound lover,
10 To beautify him, only lacks a cover.
The fish lives in the sea – and 'tis much pride
For fair without the fair within to hide.
That book in many's eyes doth share the glory
That in gold clasps locks in the golden story.
15 So shall you share all that he doth possess
By having him, making yourself no less.
NURSE
No less? Nay, bigger! Women grow by men.
LADY CAPULET
Speak briefly: can you like of Paris' love?
JULIET
I'll look to like, if looking liking move.
20 But no more deep will I endart mine eye
Than your consent gives strength to make it fly.

Starting with this extract, explore how Shakespeare presents marriage in *Romeo and Juliet*.

Write about:
- how Shakespeare presents marriage in this extract
- how Shakespeare presents marriage in the play as a whole.

(30 marks)
AO4 (4 marks)

Unit 8 Write your response to this question, focusing on using relevant contextual information.

Answers

Unit 1

Page 3

1 a/b

N Escalus, Prince of Verona

C ~~Paris~~ [killed by Romeo]

M Lord Montague

C Lord Capulet

M Romeo

M Benvolio

M Lady Montague

M ~~Mercutio~~ [killed by Tybalt]

C ~~Tybalt~~ [killed by Romeo]

N Friar Lawrence

C Sampson

C Nurse

C Juliet

M Lady Montague

C Lady Capulet

N Friar John

C Gregory

M Abraham

2 a three times

b–e Sunday day: Montagues/Capulets fight in the square

Sunday night: Romeo and Juliet meet at the Capulet ball/fall in love

Monday day: Romeo and Juliet meet at Friar Lawrence's cell and marry/Tybalt kills Mercutio in a street fight/Romeo kills Tybalt to avenge his friend's death

Monday night: Romeo and Juliet spend the night together

Tuesday: Romeo leaves for Mantua/Juliet is told to marry Paris

Tuesday night: Juliet takes 'poison'

Wednesday morning: Juliet is found 'dead'/Romeo hears Juliet is dead

Wednesday night: Romeo kills Paris, not knowing who he is/Romeo takes poison/Juliet wakes, finds Romeo dead and stabs herself with his dagger

Thursday: The two families make peace

Page 4

1 For example (killing of Tybalt):

a Causes: Juliet's mother urges her to marry Paris; Benvolio persuades Romeo to go to the ball and test his feelings for Rosaline; Romeo and Juliet fall in love at first sight before finding out they are from opposing families; Romeo and Juliet are married in secret by Friar Lawrence.

b Consequences: Benvolio is questioned about the fight and Romeo is banished; Friar Lawrence's plan fails when his message does not get to Romeo; Romeo kills Paris then kills himself by taking poison.

Page 5

1 Romeo would not have killed Tybalt and therefore would not have been banished. Arguably, Mercutio, as a more light-hearted character, might have been able to help Romeo make peace with the Capulets, thus preventing the later deaths.

2 a/b For example: [significance = 3] Juliet refuses to marry Paris so her father threatens to disown her; relevant as it shows parent–child conflict.

Page 6

1 The student has shown they understand where the extract comes from in the play, considered the impact of the extract on later events and used that to show how it relates to conflict.

Page 7

1 a 1.2; 1.5; 2.6; 3.4; 3.5 [1]; 4.1; 5.2

b For example: 3.1 [both]; 3.5 [2]

c For example: 3.1 [1] – violent conflict; 3.5 [2] – family conflict

Page 8

Responses could focus on:

Romeo's anguish in:

- Act 1 Scenes 1 & 2: Romeo is lovesick about Rosaline
- Act 1 Scene 4: Mercutio urges Romeo not to give in to the anguish of love
- Act 3 Scene 1: Romeo regrets his cowardice after Mercutio's death
- Act 5 Scene 3: [extract] Romeo realises he has killed Paris

Juliet's anguish in:

- Act 3 Scene 2: Juliet is conflicted over the death of Tybalt
- Act 3 Scene 5: Juliet refuses to marry Paris
- Act 5 Scene 4: Juliet agonises about taking the potion

Unit 2

Page 11

1 a 4(A), 6(B), 3(C) are arguably the most relevant.

b A: Juliet has a vision of Romeo dead, which suggests that his death is foretold and they are controlled by fate.

B: Juliet is a pessimist who thinks it is unfair that fate seems to control her life.

C: Romeo seems to feel he has some control over his life as he thinks they will meet again.

Page 12

1 For example:

  a JULIET
  Do you think we will meet again?
  ROMEO
  I'm sure we will and then all these troubles will be
  Nice stories we can tell in the future.
  JULIET
  Oh dear, I am a real pessimist about things!
  I think I can see you below me
  Like somebody dead in a tomb:
  Either my eyes are weak, or you look pale.

  b Romeo tries to reassure Juliet that they will meet again, but she is worried as she has a vision of him dead.

  c It suggests fate is controlling their futures as the audience knows that Romeo will die.

  d 'O God, I have an ill-divining soul!' 'As one dead in the bottom of a tomb.'

2 **a** For example:
  - Juliet is begging fate to let Romeo come back.
  - She feels fate has been unfair to her so far.
  - People believe fate is controlling their lives and can be unfair.

  b For example: 'All men call thee fickle'.

Page 13

1 All except E are valid.

2 For example: D, A, C, F, B

3 <u>In this extract</u> [D] Shakespeare presents fate as something very negative. <u>For example,</u> [A] Juliet has a vision of Romeo's death: 'Methinks I see thee, now thou art so low/As one dead in the bottom of a tomb.' <u>This suggests that</u> [C] ideas about fate in 'Romeo and Juliet' are linked to death. <u>Also,</u> [F] Juliet is worried that her vision is going to come true as she thinks Romeo 'look'st pale'. <u>This emphasises that</u> [B] Juliet feels that fate is controlling their lives.

4 **a** Key point: D
  b Evidence: A, F
  c Comment: C, B
  d Response: D

Page 14

1 **a** The student has achieved all of the criteria.

  b *In this extract,* [plot] *where Romeo and Juliet say goodbye as he has been banished,* [response] *they are shown to have different reactions to the role of fate in their lives.* [relevance/key point] *Romeo is presented as the more positive of the lovers* [evidence] *as he tries to reassure Juliet that their 'woes' will turn into 'sweet discourses in our time to come',* [comment] *suggesting that he believes he has some control over their future.* [relevance/key point] *Juliet, on the other hand, is more negative and links fate to death* [evidence] *by talking of a vision of Romeo 'As one dead in the bottom of a tomb.'* [comment] *This suggests that Romeo's death is his destiny and nothing can stop it happening,* [response] *which presents fate as something controlling the characters' lives.*

Page 16

Responses could focus on:
- Romeo's conflicted feelings about Paris: 'Said he not so? Or did I dream it so?'
- Romeo's worry about his sanity: 'Or am I mad'
- Romeo's feelings of guilt and being misused by fate: 'One writ with me in sour misfortune's book! I'll bury thee in a triumphant grave. –'
- Romeo's anguish at finding Juliet dead: 'Death, that hath sucked the honey of thy breath,/Hath had no power yet upon thy beauty.'

Unit 3

Page 19

1 **a** tyrannous; rough **b** tyrannous – oppressive/controlling/dictatorial/savage; rough – harsh/bumpy/brutal

  c Shakespeare's choice of words suggests love can be pleasant and kind, but might also be harsh and painful.

2 **a** Personification ('love . . see') and oxymoron ('loving hate')

  b 'O brawling love, O loving hate' – oxymorons that suggest love is both wonderful and violent.

Page 20

1 For example:

  a Romeo: despondent – consumed with romantic love and cannot think of anything else.
  Benvolio: sympathetic/kind – wants to help.
  Their friendship: strong/brotherly – Benvolio anticipates Romeo's response.
  Romantic love: painful – easy to fall in and out of.

  b The short lines emphasise the sharp, painful feelings of falling in and out of love.

2 **a** Romeo
  b It suggests he is the more romantic and also the more immature of the two.
  c Benvolio's
  d It suggests he is the more practical of the two.

Page 21

1 A – b; B – d; C – e; D – a; E – c

2 For example: 'O heavy lightness, serious vanity' is an oxymoron that suggests love appears to be something you can take lightly, but is really something that will take over your life and make you think about nothing but yourself.

Page 22

key point focusing on the key words in the question/a response to the question	In this extract romantic love is presented as painful and cruel.
evidence from the text to support the point	First, there is an exchange of several short lines between Benvolio and Romeo where Benvolio finishes Romeo's sentences with questions: 'In love?/Out –/Of love?'.
comments on the evidence and its impact/a comment on structural choice(s)	The short, sharp structure of these lines introduces the idea that falling in and out of love can hurt.
short quotations as evidence of language choices/ use of subject terminology	Benvolio then emphasises this negative side of romantic love by personifying it as something 'gentle' to look at but 'tyrannous' in reality.
a comment on language choice(s)	This suggests that love can be pleasant, as 'gentle' has connotations of kindness and understanding. However, Shakespeare's use of the adjective 'tyrannous' suggests that love is really very harsh and controlling, causing suffering and oppression.

Page 24

Responses could focus on the Nurse as a practical character:

- 'Faith, here it is': straightforward language
- 'Romeo's a dishclout to him': very basic, ordinary language
- 'I think it best you married with the County' – gives practical advice

Unit 4

Page 27

(1) romantic: R & J; immature: R; innocent: J; foolish: R; impulsive: R; depressed: R; obedient: J

(2) All responses are arguable as each marks a step in the character's development.

Page 28

(1) (a) For example: A – c; B – b; C – e; D – g; E – a; F – d; G – f

(b) For example: The servants meeting in the street shows that loyalty to the family includes even the lowest in status.

(2) (a) For example: When Gregory and Sampson exchange insults with the Montague servants, the conflict is verbal and shown as bawdy and comic as they tell rude jokes.

(b) For example: The theme of conflict starts off being shown in a light-hearted way when the servants trade jokes, but then becomes more violent and dramatic when Tybalt and Mercutio fight in the street. Conflict is finally shown to be tragic as the families' feud ultimately causes the deaths of Romeo and Juliet.

Page 29

(1) (a) For example:
When we are first introduced to Juliet in Act 1 Scene 3, she is with her nurse and shows no interest in love or getting married, but does agree to think about marrying Paris. This presents her as both <u>innocent</u> and <u>obedient</u>.

When she meets Romeo in Act 1 Scene 5, she encourages his romantic attention. This presents her as <u>becoming more independent</u>.

Then, in Act 2 Scene 2, she is presented as becoming more <u>daring</u> when she suggests marrying Romeo in secret the next day.

Later in the play, when <u>she refuses to marry Paris after Tybalt has been killed,</u> she is shown as <u>disobedient and disrespectful</u>.

(b) For example: When she has woken from the potion-induced sleep and found Romeo dead, Juliet is presented as alone and courageous as she decides to kill herself.

(2) (a) i – C; ii – A; iii – D; iv – E

(b) For example: Loyalty is first presented in a comic way as the servants remain loyal to their families. However, it becomes a more serious matter as the play progresses because it is loyalty to his friend Mercutio that causes Romeo to kill Tybalt.

Page 30

Juliet is first presented to the audience through her father, who tells Paris that she is too young to marry at only fourteen. [scene 1.2] Juliet then appears, accompanied by first her nurse and then her nurse and her mother [scene 1.3], which emphasises her youth and immaturity [comment]. Shakespeare presents her as innocent and child-like as she has no interest in marriage, declaring it an 'honour that I dream not of' [comment]. At this point she is not presented as disobedient [comment], as she agrees to consider Paris as a suitor, and even says she will not go further than her mother would approve of.

However, Juliet is soon shown to be more independent than these early scenes suggest [development]. Although Romeo starts their relationship, Juliet does encourage him by responding to his kiss at her family's ball [scene 1.5] and she is presented as knowing her own mind [comment] as she declares her love for him in the balcony scene [scene 2.2]. This suggests she is becoming rebellious [development] as she knows that he is an enemy of her family [comment].

Page 32

Responses could focus on:

- the Nurse as a surrogate mother to Juliet: in Act 1 Scene 3, she talks about knowing her since she was born
- the Nurse as a comic figure: in Act 2 Scene 4, she is mocked by the Montagues in the street
- the Nurse as serious: in Act 2 Scene 4, she warns Romeo not to hurt Juliet

Unit 5

Page 35

1 **a** Romeo: feels revenge is necessary and justified as he is ashamed of his cowardly behaviour. Benvolio: feels Romeo has been foolish to take revenge and it could be dangerous.

b For example: The reactions of both characters suggest that although revenge can appear to be justified, it is also foolish and dangerous.

2 **a/b** All are arguably valid.

Page 36

1 **a** All are arguably valid.

b For example: A 1.1; B 3.1 (both); C 3.5/5.3; D Prologue; E Prologue

2 **a/b** For example: When the Capulet servants taunt the Montague servants, it shows that revenge is related to family honour as it leads to Tybalt wanting revenge for the insults.

Page 37

1 B, A, C, D

2 **a** For example: A, B, C, D (i.e. focus first on Tybalt, then Romeo, then Juliet)

b For example: B, C, A, D (i.e. focus first on avoiding revenge, then revenge as foolish, last on danger)

Page 38

1 **a** Either A or C is valid.

b chronologically

Page 40

Responses could focus on:

(in the extract)

- Friar Lawrence's irritation at Romeo's lack of clarity: 'Riddling confession finds but riddling shrift.'
- his amusement at Romeo's quick change of heart, for example:
  - 'Holy Saint Francis, what a change is here!' – use of saint's name suggests he is relaxed about religion
  - 'How much salt water thrown away in waste, To season love, that of it doth not taste!'
- his wisdom: 'For doting, not for loving, pupil mine.'

(in the play as a whole)

- Friar Lawrence's motive is to unite the two families: in Act 2 Scene 6, he marries the lovers in secret
- Friar Lawrence as wise/learned:
  - in Act 2 Scene 3, he advises Romeo not to be hasty
  - in Act 4 Scene 1, he knows what herbs to give Juliet
- Friar Lawrence as trustworthy: in Act 3 Scene 3, he shelters Romeo when he is banished
- Friar Lawrence ultimately fails: in Act 5 Scene 3, he fails to stop Juliet killing herself and then faces no consequences

Unit 6

Page 43

1 **a** At this point Lady Capulet is shown to be a <u>distant</u> parent.

b <u>Important</u> ideas about parental love are shown at this point in the play.

2 **a** 3.1 [1]: Romeo; 3.2: Juliet; 3.5: Lord Capulet

b 3.1 [1]: honour; 3.1 [2]: fate; 3.2: love; 3.3: wisdom; 3.5: family conflict

3 **a** For example: A and B

b For example: A – conflict (Romeo denying his family will cause conflict)

c For example: '<u>Deny thy father</u> and <u>refuse thy name</u>'

Page 44

1 Key event: For example: Juliet shows defiance by telling her mother she is not ready for marriage.

Key quotation: For example: 'I will not marry yet.'

2 Examples are likely to focus on Juliet's refusal to marry Paris and the parents' grief at the end of the play.

3 E, F, G and H are all valid.

4 Using both key events and quotations is likely to be the most effective approach.

Page 45

1 **b** For example: The audience is expected to like Lord Capulet at this point because he seems concerned and caring.

2 For example:

A Romeo is suffering from unrequited love of Rosaline but his parents do not know what is making him so sad.

B Lord Montague says Romeo is 'so secret and so close', which suggests he does not know his son very well.

C However, he shows concern, which suggests that he cares about his son's happiness.

D This suggests a loving parent–child relationship.

E This would encourage the audience to like Lord Montague.

Page 46

When Juliet refuses to marry Paris after the death of Tybalt,	uses a key event as evidence
Before storming off in a rage,	explains the context of the evidence
he calls her a 'young baggage' and tells her to 'hang, beg, starve, die in the streets' and then talks of disowning her completely.	uses quotations as evidence
The word 'baggage' suggests she is just an unwanted possession rather than his daughter and the use of harsh verbs such as 'beg' and 'starve' shows the strength of his feelings.	analysis comment on the writer's choice of language and/or structure

Lord Capulet shows himself to be a harsh and domineering parent.	analysis comment on character
That makes Lord Capulet seem to be the villain.	
This would make the audience start to hate him.	analysis comment on Shakespeare's intention
At this point, Shakespeare is showing a complete breakdown in parent–child relations.	analysis comment on theme

Page 48

See the suggested answers for page 40 above.

Unit 7

Page 51

1. a. Beginning: feud/fate/conflict/threat;
   Middle: romance/marriage/conflict/revenge/banishment; End: advice/plan/suicide
   b. For example: At the point when Romeo kills Tybalt as they know he might then be executed.
2. For example:
   a.
   - Juliet falls in love and then discovers Romeo is a Montague.
   - Friar Lawrence's letter to Romeo never arrives.

   b. For example: Shakespeare uses the idea of fate to create anticipation for the audience, as they know from the start that things are not going to go smoothly. This means they spend the play wondering how and when the tragic events are going to happen.

Page 52

1. a. A – d; B – c; C – b; D – a
   b. For example:
   Mercutio jokes with Benvolio before he fights with Tybalt and is killed.
   The Nurse is teased by the Montagues before she speaks to Romeo about the marriage.
2. a. When Romeo and Juliet first meet, the audience knows they are from two feuding families, but they themselves do not.
   When Romeo refuses to fight Tybalt, the audience knows that it is because he is now married to Tybalt's cousin.
   b. When Romeo refuses to fight Tybalt, it is dramatic for the audience as they expect the hot-headed Mercutio to get angry, and for Tybalt to be insulted when his challenge is not accepted. They expect some form of conflict, which they know will be dangerous because the Prince has banned further violence.

Page 53

1. a/b A and C or B and D are both valid.
2. a/b For example:
   Another instance of reckless behaviour is when Juliet defies her father and refuses to marry Paris. Juliet's father wants her to marry without delay, but she asks him to show 'patience' and begs him to listen. *This is an example of dramatic irony as the audience knows that she is already married to Romeo so they would anticipate serious conflict at this point. Juliet started the play as an innocent, child-like character but the way she stands up to her parents shows that she is rapidly developing into an independent young woman. As the audience already knows the ending of the play will be tragic, this reckless behaviour would add excitement to the unfolding of the plot.*

Page 54

1. By opening the play in this way, with the servants rather than with important characters, Shakespeare is showing how significant the feud is as it obviously affects all levels of society. / By starting the play in this way, Shakespeare suggests that all parts of Verona society are capable of reckless behaviour. This violence would make the audience tense, as this scene comes immediately after the Prologue warns that 'new mutiny' will end in tragedy.
2. The most obvious type of reckless behaviour in Romeo and Juliet is that which leads to violent conflict. / By starting the play in this way, Shakespeare suggests that all parts of Verona society are capable of reckless behaviour
3. For example: The play starts with the Capulet servant, Sampson, boasting of what he will do to the Montagues.

Page 56

Key events could include:
- opening scene of argument/fight that starts with servants
- Tybalt's anger when he sees Romeo at the ball
- the deaths of Mercutio and Tybalt, followed by Romeo's banishment
- Juliet's argument with her father after refusing to marry Paris
- the deaths of Romeo and Juliet.

Key structural points could include:
- Juliet realising Romeo is a Montague *after* she has fallen in love with him
- dramatic irony – the audience knows Romeo is married to Juliet and that is why he refuses to fight Tybalt, despite hating him.

Unit 8

Page 59

1. All are relevant except A, B, F and G.
2. Romeo – K; Juliet – H/I/J; The death of Mercutio – D/K; Paris asking to marry Juliet – H/I; The opening fight scene – D

Page 60

1. a. A identifies the time in which the play was written and a relevant attitude.

   B identifies the time in which the play was written and a relevant situation at that time.

   C identifies the time in which the play was written and a relevant attitude at that time; also considers the impact on an audience and compares today's audience with Shakespeare's.

- **b** C is the most detailed, developed comment on context.
- **2 a** Responses are likely to focus on the impact of Lady Capulet's distant mothering on a modern audience in comparison with sixteenth-century acceptance of this attitude.

Page 61

- **1 a** Sentences A–D focus on impact; Sentences a–d focus on context.
  - **b** d is relevant to A; a is relevant to B; b is relevant to C; c is relevant to D
  - **c** Any two combinations from **b** above would be valid.

Page 62

When Lord Capulet hears Juliet's refusal to marry Paris, he becomes very angry,	uses a key event as evidence
first asking why 'Doth she not give thanks?', then insulting her: 'you green-sickness carrion', and then threatening her: 'My fingers itch'.	uses a quotation as evidence
This is a very disturbing moment in the play for a modern audience as it suggests he feels physical force against his daughter is acceptable.	comments on the impact of the evidence
However, because Shakespeare's audience lived in a patriarchal society, where men were in total control of their families,	identifies a relevant contextual point
they would be more shocked by Juliet's disobedience.	explores the audience's response in the light of this contextual point
When Lord Capulet hears Juliet's refusal to marry Paris, he becomes very angry,	explores Shakespeare's intention in the light of this contextual point

Page 64

Responses could focus on:

- the relationship of Lord and Lady Capulet: he is head of the house and she follows his orders (Act 3 Scene 4); very patriarchal, typical of Elizabethan society
- arranged marriage: Lord Capulet wants Juliet to be happy (turns down Paris in Act 1 Scene 3), but still gives her no choice when she refuses later (Act 3 Scene 5); young women were expected to marry to improve family status
- happy marriage is presented as unusual: Romeo and Juliet marry in secret

Unit 9

Page 67

1 a–c For example:

		Character	Audience
1.1	Romeo tells Benvolio he is suffering from unrequited love	Benvolio – amused idealistic/unrealistic	sentiment
1.3	The Nurse recalls events of Juliet's life	Nurse – verbose nurturing/sentimental	amusement
2.2	The balcony scene	Romeo – impulsive fairy tale/romantic	affection
3.1	Romeo decides to fight Tybalt	Tybalt – arrogant honourable/conflicted	anticipation
5.3	Romeo and Juliet are found dead	Lord Capulet – despairing eternal/doomed	sorrow

Page 68

- **1 a** when; whereas, and; because, so
  - **b** All version 'B's use conjunctions to express the relationship between the two clauses more clearly.
- **2** The Nurse seems excited to see Romeo and Juliet falling in love, and acts as their go-between, <u>although</u> she does warn Romeo not to hurt Juliet.

  <u>Although</u> Juliet refuses to marry her father's choice of husband, Paris is presented as a suitable husband.

  Lady Capulet is dismissive of Juliet's grief for Tybalt, <u>whereas</u> Lord Capulet is caring and compares her to a small boat in a storm.

Page 69

- **1** For example:
  - **a** Mercutio is killed by Tybalt with a hidden thrust under Romeo's arm <u>and</u> curses both families before he dies.
  - **b** Mercutio is killed by Tybalt with a hidden thrust under Romeo's arm, <u>causing</u> Romeo to want to avenge his death.
  - **c** Mercutio is killed by Tybalt with a hidden thrust under Romeo's arm, <u>which</u> causes Romeo to feel guilty.
- **2** Mercutio often repeats Romeo's words and makes bawdy jokes, <u>encouraging</u> the audience to see him as light-hearted.

  The letter from Friar Lawrence fails to reach Romeo in Mantua, <u>which creates</u> the impression that fate is again controlling the young lovers' lives.

Page 70

1 a–d For example:

Once she has married Romeo, Juliet is presented as <u>courageous when</u> she refuses to marry Paris. Juliet <u>challenges</u> her father <u>when</u> he gets angry <u>and</u> calls her a 'baggage', <u>presenting</u> him as a <u>domineering</u> father. The audience would <u>enjoy</u> this as they would <u>empathise with</u> Juliet. Juliet's Nurse then tells her to marry Paris, <u>so</u> Juliet sends her away, <u>which creates the impression</u> that she is now <u>vulnerable</u> but <u>also</u> brave.

Notes